S0-AOQ-401

Career Launcher

Food Services

Career Launcher series

Advertising and Public Relations
Computers and Programming
Education
Energy
Fashion
Film
Finance
Food Services
Health Care Management
Health Care Providers
Hospitality
Internet
Law
Law Enforcement and Public Safety
Manufacturing
Nonprofit Organizations
Performing Arts
Professional Sports Organizations
Real Estate
Recording Industry
Television
Video Games

Career Launcher

Food Services

Kelly Kagamas Tomkies

Ferguson Publishing
An imprint of Infobase Publishing

Career Launcher: Food Services

Copyright © 2010 by Infobase Publishing, Inc.

Ferguson
An imprint of Infobase Publishing
132 West 31st Street
New York NY 10001

331.7647
TU58f

Library of Congress Cataloging-in-Publication Data

Tomkies, Kelly Kagamas.
  Food services / by Kelly Kagamas Tomkies. — 1st ed.
    p. cm. — (Career launcher)
  Includes bibliographical references and index.
  ISBN-13: 978-0-8160-7967-4 (hardcover : alk. paper)
  ISBN-10: 0-8160-7967-6 (hardcover : alk. paper)
  1. Food service—Vocational guidance. I. Title.
  TX911.2.T68 2010
  647.95′023—dc22

                                                           2009028106

Ferguson books are available at special discounts when purchased in bulk quantities for businesses, associations, institutions, or sales promotions. Please call our Special Sales Department in New York at (212) 967-8800 or (800) 322-8755.

You can find Ferguson on the World Wide Web at http://www.fergpubco.com

Produced by Print Matters, Inc.
Text design by A Good Thing, Inc.
Cover design by Takeshi Takahashi
Cover printed by Art Print Company, Taylor, PA
Book printed and bound by Maple Press, York, PA
Date printed: May 2010

Printed in the United States of America

10 9 8 7 6 5 4 3 2 1

This book is printed on acid-free paper.

Contents

Foreword

Restaurants are an industry unlike any other. There is no industry that reaches so deeply into the heart of this country, touches so many people, embodies so many dreams, provides so many livelihoods, and offers so much community as America's restaurants.

Every one of the nearly 1 million restaurants and food-service operations in the United States enhances the quality of life for all they serve. Each has regular customers; some have hundreds. All of these regulars have a favorite booth or dish or server that makes them feel good no matter how they felt when they walked in the door.

Restaurants are not just the heart of our neighborhoods. They are the backbone of our national, state, and local economies. Restaurant sales account for 4 percent of our nation's gross domestic product. Restaurant businesses serve more than 130 million customers each and every day. Every dollar spent in a restaurant generates another $2 in sales for related industries, bringing their total impact on the economy to more than $1.5 trillion a year. Restaurants are America's gathering place—and there is a vibrant place in that industry for those who wish to be there.

In 2009, restaurants will employ 13 million people, about 1 in 10 working Americans. They are the nation's second-largest private-sector employer. Over the next 10 years, restaurant and food service operations will be hiring 1.8 million new employees, many in management positions. Is it possible for any hard-working individual to be one of the industry's next success stories? Absolutely!

It is not an uncommon story for professionals in the industry to go from the dish room to the boardroom. With determination, creativity, and a love for hospitality, people in this industry can start at the entry-level and quickly move up into positions of prominence.

Most readers of this book have probably already had a taste of working in the restaurant and food service industry—nearly one-half of all adults have worked in restaurants! For 1 in 4 people, it was their very first job. Even those who have not worked in a restaurant before can readily see the variety of opportunities available. Whether someone has dreams of becoming a chef-operator, the master manager of a multinational chain, the creator of the next great marketing campaign, or an innovative designer or architect, there is a career in the restaurant industry that matches that dream.

In this industry, it is not as much about whom you know and where you have been as it is about who you are and what you can do. It is about a person's energy, creativity, work ethic, and style with people. A person who works hard and stays committed to the industry can do very well. If this person then chooses to leave the industry, the skills first learned there will help him or her do well nearly anywhere else. Throughout our history, restaurants have offered countless families with big dreams the chance to express their creativity and serve their communities.

The entrepreneurial opportunity in the industry is remarkable, and the career options are multiplying. As a nation, we are spending more of our income eating out. This year, we will spend nearly half of every food dollar on food prepared outside the home, according to the most recent research conducted by the National Restaurant Association.

Today there are roughly 90 cooking shows on TV, across nine different networks. The Food Network alone has broadcast more than 200 shows on how to make a hamburger—meaning even the basic burger has been taken to a whole new level. So we respect a good burger when we get one.

In the last 10 years, the number of cooking schools has nearly doubled. Five of America's most popular magazines by circulation are food magazines. It is clear we love our food. Our interest in cooking has only intensified our interest in *someone else's* cooking as well as our own. This has created more and better educational and career opportunities. So now is your chance to seize these opportunities that the restaurant and food service industry can provide.

Whatever your interest, whatever your passion, there is a path to follow—or create. From front-of-the-house service and management to culinary finesse, there is a place for everyone. Whether the attraction is to real estate, finance, science, or technology, the food service industry needs employees with the talent, skills, and passion to perform. If the fascination lies with marketing, communications, advertising, or design, there are opportunities in this industry for people with those skills and interests.

The National Restaurant Association is committed to helping the industry see what's around the corner in four critical areas: food and healthy living, jobs and careers, entrepreneurship and profitability, and sustainability and stewardship. The association is doing all it can to support this remarkable industry, whether by serving up research and insights, offering scholarships for hospitality students, or providing best-in-class food-safety training to industry professionals.

Together with the National Restaurant Association Educational Foundation, the association's vision is to lead America's restaurant industry into a new era of prosperity, prominence, and participation, enhancing the quality of life for all we serve. I look forward to welcoming you to the industry.

—Dawn Sweeney
PRESIDENT AND CEO
NATIONAL RESTAURANT ASSOCIATION
WASHINGTON, D.C.

Acknowledgments

I would like to sincerely thank the following people for their efforts to provide me with information, contacts, and interviews for this book:

- All of the wonderful people at the National Restaurant Association, especially Dawn Sweeney, president and CEO and Brice Grindy, senior economist
- Francine Cohen, editor in chief, *Food & Beverage Magazine*
- Victor Gielisse, associate vice president, Culinary Institute of America
- Jim Grote, founder and CEO of Donato's Pizza
- Karen Ickes, senior vice president of human resources, Wendy's International
- Clint R. Lautenschleger, director of staffing at Bob Evans Farms, Inc.
- Chef Dave Martin, Vynl Restaurants, New York City
- Edna Morris, CEO of Geshai Ollin and a founding member of The Women's Foodservice Forum
- Mario Ponce, principal, Partners in Hospitality
- Ed Rothenberg, vice president of strategy and innovations, Micros Systems Inc.

Introduction

As a child you discover things you like to do. You try different activities, learn new skills, and have a lot of fun. Somewhere along the way you figure out what you want to do when you "grow up." While you can go to college, work in your chosen industry, and even get sound advice from established professionals, at some point you want a how-to manual that gives you solid advice for succeeding in your chosen profession.

This is where the Career Launchers series comes in. While no book can encapsulate everything you need to know about a particular industry, this book endeavors to put together a package of information that will give you a historical perspective, the key trends, a snapshot of the industry, an idea of the job opportunities available, tips for success, and resources you can use throughout your career.

This book is written for the new professional. Whether you just graduated from culinary school, received your degree in hospitality and landed that manager's position, or are starting your own restaurant, you will have lots of questions. Career Launchers may not have *all* the answers, but you will find this book loaded with enough information that if you cannot find the answers in its pages, you will definitely know where to go to find it outside of them.

You can use this book as a handy reference guide. If on your first day on the job someone throws an unfamiliar term at you, turn to "Talk Like a Pro" and look it up. If you are wondering if you should join an industry association or attend a conference, you can turn to the "Resources" chapter for more information. You can also use the book to find solid advice from industry veterans and executives who have "been there and done that."

You can never have too much knowledge. Career Launchers gives you the basic knowledge you need to launch a successful career in the food services industry. As a former editor of a publication called *Midwest Food Service News*, I already knew that the food services industry's executives are some of the most helpful and community-minded people in the country. As any newcomer to the industry will very quickly learn, even competitors in the restaurant and food services industry like to help each other. All it took was one e-mail mentioning the book to one person, and several people called, e-mailed, or sent names of others whose expertise would be an excellent addition to the book. Throughout the pages of this book, one of the leading sources of information is the National Restaurant Association. Through this excellent organization access was gained to member-only reports and information; in addition, the association president and CEO Dawn Sweeney graciously accepted the invitation to write the foreword.

This industry is overflowing with knowledge and those who are willing to share it with others. Finding books, articles, and scheduling interviews with industry veterans and experts was not difficult.

The process used to write this book was fairly simple. Looking at the goals for each chapter, as much information as possible was gathered pertaining to the subject matter. The resources used were primarily textbooks, books, articles, and academic papers and studies. Countless hours were spent searching the Internet and reading books and other materials to gather the information for the "Talk Like a Pro," "On the Job," and "Industry Resources" chapters. Dozens of industry experts were e-mailed and called, and phone interviews were scheduled, asking questions about the hottest trends, the biggest opportunities, and information on how to succeed. Chefs, teachers, restaurant owners, and executives generously donated their time and their thoughts so readers would be privy to their hard-earned knowledge and experience. Most of these sources have learned their lessons the hard way, and they are eager to spare new generations the pain of making the same mistakes.

There are many facets of the food services industry. Not surprisingly, commercial restaurants make up more than 60 percent of it, so this book is decidedly restaurant-focused. But even readers who are working in a noncommercial food service operation, as personal chefs, or are employed by a company that supplies products to the industry will find the information in this book helpful. The "Tips for Success" chapter certainly applies to many industries. The "Industry History" chapter provides an excellent background for how the industry got to where it is today, and the "State of the Industry" chapter is a great tool to use when targeting customers.

Of course, like all professions, food services is rapidly changing. What is hot today will be yesterday's news tomorrow. So if there is one overriding theme in this book, it is the need to stay current. Do not let learning about the industry end here. Utilize the resources listed in this book and read other books, buy subscriptions to trade publications, sign up for association alerts, e-newsletters, and podcasts, and attend conferences and seminars. Stay informed.

As mentioned before, the information about this industry is amazingly abundant. When it came to the history of the industry there were a few paths that could be taken. There was an extraordinary amount of information available about the histories of certain foods. In fact, as many readers may already know, there are professional food historians and entire encyclopedias of foods, where they came from, when, and how they developed.

Then there was the very interesting path of how food service organizations and systems actually started, when, and how. Although this book deals with the industry in the United States, its early beginnings took place across the ocean in Europe.

Readers will find that the end result in Chapter 1, "Industry History," is the interweaving of all three paths. The history of certain foods and beverages like hamburgers, ice cream, coffee, and soft drinks, all had an impact on the development of restaurants. Readers will find some of their histories included in this chapter. The main focus though, is the second path, how food services systems started first in Europe, and then in the United States. Readers will also see that the latter part of the chapter deals quite a bit with drive-in and fast-food restaurants, since they do make up a large part of the industry today.

What is not contained in the history chapter is a history of noncommercial and supplier organizations, although the beginnings of food preservation and processing are mentioned. All food service operations owe their beginnings, at least in part, to colleges and university food service systems, and this is mentioned in the chapter.

In Chapter 2, "State of the Industry," please note again that the primary focus of the chapter is the restaurant industry. That is not to say that noncommercial and other segments are not discussed in the chapter; they are. But since the restaurant segment constitutes the majority of operations in the industry, most of the focus is on it. Again, a lot of the information contained in the chapter will be useful to anyone in the industry, especially suppliers. Gaining a more thorough knowledge of restaurant customers can only help those supplying them serve them more effectively.

The information in the remaining chapters is easily applied to any segment of the industry. "On the Job" opens the doors to new horizons and careers in the industry of which readers may not have been aware. "Tips for Success" offers information on how to build a professional reputation, increase the chances of getting promoted, hunt for jobs and interview, and develop a career path. "Talk Like a

Pro" is a glossary of industry terms. Some of them might be heard on the job every day. Others may only be heard in passing a few times a year, but if a term comes up that is unrecognizable there is a good chance it can be found in the glossary. The "Resources" chapter helps readers learn where to go for more information about the industry. It includes books, associations, educational resources, publications, and Web sites. If there is a gap in anyone's knowledge base, the "Resources" chapter can point him or her in the right direction to fill it.

Finally, there are special boxed features spread throughout the book. These features may provide some handy fast facts related to the chapter or industry, offer a more detailed look at industry technology, or offer other insights and useful information. Look for these special boxed features throughout each chapter.

While each chapter in *Career Launchers: Food Services* presents different information about the food services industry, there are some common ideas and thoughts throughout. One interesting fact to keep in mind is that while this is one of the largest industries in the country in terms of sales and employees, it is not for everyone. It is a service industry, which means employees work when people want service.

Let's take, for example, a person who works for Starbucks. She arrives at work at 5:00 A.M. If someone does not show up for the next shift at 10:00 A.M. she may be asked to stay. Early in the morning customers are not always bright-eyed and bushy-tailed. She has had her share of dealing with unfriendly and downright rude people, and all the while she maintains a positive, courteous attitude. Most days she is on her feet the whole day and when she gets home she cannot wait to take a shower because she smells like coffee and bread. Her story is not unusual. But at the end of the day if you ask her what she likes about it, it comes back to one thing: the people. Despite the few rude ones who come her way, there are the regulars who know her by name. She sees them when she is not at work and they are happy to see her and stop and chat.

Nearly every industry expert interviewed mentioned how important relationships are in this business. If someone does not like working with people, then he or she had better take a back-office position, and even then he or she had better appreciate how important customers are to the business. Readers will find in nearly every chapter of the book how important it is to have a passion for food and serving people. Without those passions, it is just another job. For anyone entering this career that has those passions, experts will promise one thing: you will *never* be bored.

Chapter 1

Industry History

The word "history" conjures up memories of high school and college days when students memorized dry facts and names that appeared to have no bearing on their day-to-day lives. But when it comes to learning everything about a chosen career field, reading about its history can serve some very important purposes. For example, the phrase "History always repeats itself" is not without some elements of truth. Let's say someone has an idea that can improve his or her company's standing in the market or bring more customers in the door. There is a good chance that another person in the past has already executed a similar idea. Knowing the history of what worked and what did not, and especially why, can save the grief of launching an idea that has already failed many times in the past. It can also inspire people to think of innovative ways to customize their ideas so that they will work.

Another important reason to read up on industry history is to understand its trends. Unless an employee has years of experience in the industry, studying its history is the next best way to pick up on important trends. Chef Dave Martin, teacher and chef at New York City's Vynl restaurants, is most well-known as a Season One contestant on Bravo TV Network's *Top Chef* and presents an example of an important trend. He says that during tough times Americans tend to turn to comfort foods. "In today's economy the fancy fluff is not working," says Martin. "People want real food that tastes good and doesn't break the pocketbook."

And lastly, the story of how the industry got to this point in time when on a typical day 130 million Americans will eat at a restaurant (according to the National Restaurant Association), is actually pretty darn interesting.

From feudal times to the arrival of the fast casual segment, this history will give you insights on why the food services industry is one of the largest in the world today and how it all happened.

Early History

Since eating is one of humankind's most basic needs, it is a natural assumption that the food services industry had a very early start. The food services industry began in Europe during the Middle Ages. In those days, a feudal lord might invite 100 of his closest friends and family members to dine at his castle; that's quite a lot of mouths to feed, and a staff of 100 was needed to prepare the food and serve the guests. Hence a system of food service had to be created.

Feudal lords were not the only ones creating a food service system. Religious orders, colleges and universities, and royal households were also developing systems to feed many hungry mouths. In England abbeys were constantly feeding large numbers of residents and people who were traveling through. In fact these abbeys provide some of the earliest examples of a detailed food services accounting system. The food operations in the abbeys were funded by laypeople in the local community, and the abbeys also grew a lot of their own food.

The royal household of the King of England is another example of an early food service operation. Feeding up to 250 people at a time, the cooking staff could be quite extensive. Cheap labor was in ample supply and the lowest-ranking cooking staff member often worked for scraps of food and a place to sleep on the floor. In those days there was not a lot of fuss about food safety. There were a lot of animals roaming in and out of the kitchen, and people who were passing through the kitchen often stuck their fingers into nearby pots and pans for a taste. Over the years, of course, people began recognizing the importance of properly preparing and storing foods. Equipment and storage solutions improved and fewer staff members were needed as a result.

Ice cream was invented in the mid-1600s, but was brought to the forefront by King Louis IV of France. Known for his lavish style of entertaining, the king was the first to serve ice cream at a banquet.

The delicious food immediately gained popularity. Until the 1850s the most popular flavor of ice cream was lemon.

Early Restaurants

The first restaurants were part of inns. In these early times there were two main reasons for hitting the road: either you were embarking on a religious pilgrimage or you were a merchant, hoping to score some sales in the villages down the road. Either way you needed a place where you could sleep and get a bite to eat. In these days travelers paid one price for both their accommodations and meals. There was no incentive for innkeepers to make the meals as tasty as possible, so the food was often uninspiring at best, and the service sloppy.

Meanwhile in America, restaurants first began in the form of taverns, where residents could go to drink a beer, the most common beverage in the country at the time. The first tavern in America was opened in Manhattan in 1642 by William Kieft, governor of New Amsterdam.

In 1750, Thomas Lepper opened his tavern, believed by some historians to have been named The Leopard. Copying an old English custom, this tavern took the idea of "today's specials" very literally. The tavern keeper offered no menu at all. Whatever meal he had prepared for his own supper, he offered to his customers for a few coins. Fraunces Tavern was opened in New York in 1762 by Sam Fraunces. Although it served both food and wine, it was better known for its wine. The tavern is still in operation today and diners can now also tour its museum.

Later, travel of a different kind—stagecoach travel—also created the need for inns and restaurants. These operations located along the stagecoach route were usually family-owned and operated and it was simpler to feed guests the same food the family ate. The meals were usually hearty and there was plenty of it to satisfy the guests. Wild game such as turkeys and geese were plentiful and found their way onto many tables during this time. In fact America became quite well-known for its quantity of meat.

Early examples of restaurants in these days are those opened in New York by Widow Bradshaw and John Snedicker. The widow's restaurant featured chicken fricassee, while Snedicker's offered asparagus dinners. While most travelers were more interested in meaty fare, Snedicker's tavern still attracted many patrons.

Fast
Facts

A Brief History of the First American Tavern

The first American tavern, built by director-general of New Netherland (of which New Amsterdam, later known as New York City, was a main territory) William Kieft, was located at the corner of Dock Street (now Pearl Street) and Coenties Slip in Manhattan. Kieft had the three-story stone tavern built so that visitors who came to the city for harvest fairs would have a place to stay. Over time, it came to serve as not only a tavern, but also a courthouse and jail. It was the official site of City Hall until a new one was built at the corner of Wall and Nassau Streets in the year 1700.

Around this time hotel owners in Europe began separating the billing of lodging and board. This led to the creation of distinct food service operations. The word "restaurant" is derived from the French word *restaurer*, which means to rest or refresh. French cook shops had developed and had quickly learned the market value of take-out service. They were licensed to prepare ragouts, or stews, for patrons to take and eat at inns or homes. These early restaurants also learned to post their menus on exterior walls or doors so hungry consumers would be tempted to stop for a meal.

The United States can thank its third President, Thomas Jefferson, for some of its food service history. Prior to his election Jefferson was a United States Minister in France. During his tenure there he was inspired by many of the country's customs and practices, including its food and cooking. Once in the White House Jefferson instituted many French culinary arts under the direction of the French chef Julien Lemaire, and a French maitre d'hotel. He also made sure two of his servants from his estate, Monticello, worked with these French experts so they could take this knowledge back to Monticello. He owned an ice cream machine so guests could enjoy the delicious treats. Jefferson loved to host dinner parties and they were nightly events during his White House days as well as when he returned home to Monticello. In fact the President spent more than his salary on food and wine while he was in office.

In the Western United States another innovation in the industry was being introduced. Cafeterias were a product of the gold rush days in the mid-1800s. Miners demanded quick service and in-and-out dining. Restaurant owners adapted to meet this demand and created the first cafeteria-style restaurants. They were hugely popular and quickly spread across the country.

Early restaurants in America were not well-known for their delicious cuisine. People preferred home-cooked meals for very good reason. Restaurants in the mid-1800s provided plain, hearty, and edible fare, but did not rise much above this in taste. American wives spent a great deal of their time and energy in producing three bountiful and tasty meals a day, and people did not have a lot of interest in venturing into restaurants for substandard food.

One very big exception to this rule was Delmonico's in New York. In the late 1820s John Delmonico, a sea captain, decided he was tired of life at sea and settled down in New York. Since he was originally from Ticino, Switzerland, which is wine country, Delmonico opened a store that offered wines by the barrel for home consumption. Business boomed so the following year John invited his brother Peter to join the business. Peter's experience was in baking, so Delmonico's began offering patrons wines, spirits, coffee, pastries, and chocolates. This concept was such a success that in 1831 the Delmonicos hired a French chef and opened a full-fledged restaurant. Patrons had never before sampled this kind of cooking. The Delmonicos also attempted to bring balance to restaurant food by offering more vegetable and salad dishes. They showed their patrons that they could do more with home-grown fruits and vegetables.

In 1832 a third member of the family, a nineteen-year-old nephew of John and Peter named Lorenzo, joined the family business, which was turning away so many customers that a second restaurant was opened. The second restaurant proved such a success that three more brothers were needed to keep them running. A fire destroyed most of the first restaurant in 1835, so a third restaurant, much larger and more ornately decorated, was built.

By this time Delmonico's had competition in the form of the Astor House restaurant. But the uniqueness and quality of Delmonico's continued to keep it the market leader and it thrived. One dish in particular that was created at Delmonico's is still served at countless restaurants today, Lobster Newberg. Ben Wenberg, a frequent customer of the restaurant, was given permission to create his own sauce for lobster in Delmonico's kitchen. The Delmonicos loved the sauce so much they put it on their menu, calling it Lobster à la Wenberg. But Wenberg fell out with the Delmonicos over a brawl he had started at the restaurant. Wenberg was out, but the dish remained and was renamed Lobster à la Newberg, which has since been shortened.

Lorenzo took over the operation of the restaurants after the death of his Uncle John in a hunting accident and the retirement of his Uncle Peter. He remained at the helm for three decades, expanding its reputation and renown. Lorenzo was considered a pioneer in the industry; he exemplified the combination of hard work and attention to detail that characterizes so many successful professionals in the industry.

A History of Popular Beverages

Another staple of the food services industry, carbonated beverages, was developed in the late 1700s and early 1800s, way before Pepsi or Coca-Cola came on the scene. Scientists had discovered the secret of creating what they called gaseous water in the late 1700s, but it was just considered a cool laboratory trick until 1809, when Joseph Hawkins patented his carbonated soda water and put it on the market in the United States. By 1832, the first marketing genius of the stuff, John Matthews, propelled soda water into a more solid market position with his slogan: "Youth as it sips its first soda experiences the sensations, which like the sensations of love, cannot be forgotten." The slogan was a bit long by today's standards, but equally as full of promises as today's advertising.

Fast Facts

The Growth of Restaurant Industry Sales Since 1970

1970: $42.8 billion
1980: $119.6 billion
1990: $239.3 billion
2000: $379.0 billion
Projected 2009: $565.9 billion
(http://www.restaurant.org)

While no one is quite sure whether soda water was first flavored by Elie Magliore Durand or Eugenie Roussel, both of Philadelphia, it is certain that they both sold flavored soda water to their customers, and that it was a huge hit. By 1849, there were 64 soda plants in the United States, and that number had nearly doubled by 1859, when it became a million dollar industry! Early popular flavors included root beer, birch beer, spruce beer, pepsin, ginger, lemon, cherry, and sarsaparilla. Nearly thirty years later, in 1886, Atlanta druggist John S. Pemberton invented a soda water that he believed would cure headaches and hangovers. He added coca leaves and cola nuts to plain water in a kettle in his backyard and sold it at his drugstore. He made a $50 profit the first year. Then he spilled some soda water into the cola and decided he liked the added zip it gave the mixture. Two years later Asa G. Candler, another druggist prone to violent headaches, purchased the formula from Pemberton for $2,000. It was Candler who recognized the non-pharmaceutical, commercial value of Coca-Cola and launched it as a beverage for pleasure.

It was also in the 1800s that Americans began their love affair with coffee. In the early days of the country England had tea to sell. It was cheap and readily available to the colonies, so tea became the beverage of choice in colonial America. The price of tea shot up during the War of 1812, and coffee was the most economical alternative. Today coffee houses like Starbucks comprise one of the most successful segments of the industry. According to 2007 figures by Technomic, a food services research and consulting company, Starbucks was number 3 in chain restaurant sales. The top two positions, respectively, were held by McDonald's and Burger King.

Early Innovations

As the industrial revolution of the 19th century brought about new innovations, people looked to technology for better, faster, and safer ways to preserve foods. In 1809, what has become modern-day food processing was invented. A Frenchman named Nicholas Appert invented vacuum-packed hermetically sealed jars for food storage. Emperor Napoleon, who had been looking for ways to stockpile food for his armies, awarded the clever inventor 12,000 francs. Canning as a system of food preservation is still used today.

In the 1850s in America, another inventor had developed a machine that could mass produce the tops and bottoms of tin cans for food storage. Henry Evans' machine was a huge time-saver for tinsmiths who could no longer keep up with the demand manually. Following Evans' machine, an unknown genius invented what was called "the joker." This machine replaced the need to hand-solder the lids onto cans. The total effect of these inventions is staggering. When producing the cans by hand, skilled tinsmiths produced 120 cans per day. Post-inventions, unskilled laborers produced 1,500 cans a day. By 1860, just before the Civil War, the annual output of the fledgling food processing industry was 5 million cans of food. Still, it is interesting to note that most of the canned products were purchased for military consumption, similar to the jars of food for Napoleon's army. It was not until World War II and later, when more women entered the workforce, that American housewives decided to partake of the convenience of processed foods. Up until that time, most women took pride in their culinary accomplishments over the lure of convenience.

Refrigeration was invented in the mid-1800s. A schoolteacher named Benjamin Nyce patented the first cold storage warehouse. Even though this invention broadened many horizons, it was not until nearly 100 years later that Americans used refrigerators in homes as they are used today. Early refrigeration was mainly used for transporting fresh foods.

Cookbooks of the mid-1800s called for incredible volumes of ingredients for everything from soups to oyster dishes. In the mid-1800s oysters were extremely popular. An example of this abundance is in Mrs. Horace Mann's cookbook, *Christianity in the Kitchen*, published in 1861. In this cookbook a recipe for cake calls for 20 eggs. The recipe also noted that the cook preparing the cake needed to beat the batter vigorously for three hours. Ouch.

Innovator Georges Escoffier

By the late 1800s French chef and author Georges Escoffier was becoming a well-known force in the Paris restaurant industry. Not only did Escoffier create techniques that are still used today, but he also introduced organization into the kitchen, creating the brigade system, a hierarchal system of kitchen roles that is still used today. Escoffier is credited with updating and simplifying more complicated French culinary arts originally created by Antoine Carême, a leader in the development of French haute cuisine. The result of Escoffier's simplification was that chefs throughout France, then Europe, and since worldwide are able to reproduce the finest cuisine for their customers. His methods are now considered essential techniques for all chefs to know. Because of Escoffier's efforts, the profession of chef became well-respected throughout the world. Escoffier's landmark cookbook/textbook, *Le Guide Culinaire*, was published in 1903 and is still used today.

The Early 20th Century: 1900 to 1939

By the early 1900s, another innovation in the restaurant industry was launched in Philadelphia. It was called an "automat" and its design was inspired by a "waiterless" restaurant in Berlin. The automat was a combination of cafeteria-style service and a vending machine. Customers moved through cafeteria-style lines, procuring their food selections by depositing coins in window cases. The automat was a popular segment of the industry through the 1930s.

It was during the early part of this century that a major food item—bread—transitioned from always being homemade to store-bought. In 1900, despite the fact the pre-baked bread had been introduced to consumers, 95 percent of the flour purchased in the United States was purchased for in-home, individual use. Just like the increased use of canned foods, however, pre-baked bread slowly gained popularity from the 1930s on, as more women joined the labor force. By 1970, only 15 percent of the flour sold in America was used to bake bread.

The early years of the 20th century was also when a popular cuisine was given its name. The term "Tex-Mex" was first coined by journalists in Texas during the 1920s, although it described residents of Texas who were of Mexican descent, rather than food. The term quickly became associated with Southwestern cuisine and stuck. Tex-Mex is not all the same, however; it varies throughout the region. Today, restaurants that serve Tex-Mex are some of the most popular in the industry.

Prohibition's Effect on the Food Services Industry

The movement that created the legislative act of Prohibition, which outlawed alcohol, also gained strength in the early 1900s. It had started out as a by-product of the Women's Christian Temperance Union (WCTU), which was organized by Frances Willard of Oberlin, Ohio, in the late 1890s. It gained significant momentum throughout the early part of the century. The WCTU felt that alcohol led people to commit other sins and crimes and that abolishing it could only help society. Many other like-minded people and organizations joined their cause. Oberlin College became the headquarters for the movement, which consolidated with similar organizations across the country to become the Anti-Saloon League of America. The cause gained a valuable ally in James Cannon Jr., a Southern Methodist clergy member who directed a women's college and published a daily newspaper in Richmond, Virginia. He was a lobbyist for the Anti-Saloon League in Washington, D.C. But the movement's success can be attributed primarily to Wayne Bidwell Wheeler, also from Oberlin College. This gentleman had proven himself an excellent Anti-Saloon League organizer and speaker, and showed great forethought, attending law school while maintaining his league activities. Wheeler had moved to Washington, D.C. by 1916, where he was general counsel for the league and represented a nationwide organization that sought the abolition of the manufacture and sale of alcohol.

The United States' entrance into World War I on April 16, 1917, delayed passage of Prohibition legislation, but the Anti-Saloon League continued putting pressure on senators and congressmen, and finally the Eighteenth Amendment was ratified in January 1919.

The California wine industry was hardest hit by Prohibition. Despite the fact that millions of wine-drinking immigrants from European countries continued to pour into the country, wine production declined because of Prohibition. Some growers switched to growing fruits and vegetables. But it did not take long before illegal drinking operations began to grow, which reversed that trend. Prohibition had successfully done away with California's number-one competitor, imported wines. Still, the demand was not necessarily for quality, but for massive quantities. Grapes that could produce the most wine per acre were chosen over tastier grapes. Wine merchants used clever means to circumvent Prohibition laws and to legally sell their products. They created what were called "bricks of Bacchus," or grape concentrate. Along with the bricks came careful instructions of what not to do, to prevent it from turning into the illegal wine, which of course served as instructions of how to "accidentally" make wine. The bricks typically displayed a large label which read: CAUTION: WILL FERMENT AND TURN INTO WINE.

Another industry affected by Prohibition was the beer industry. Beer was America's alcoholic drink of choice, far more preferred than wine. Since fortunately beer was big business in America at that time, its manufacturers had enough cash to wait out the dry

Keeping
in Touch

Communicating with Customers Through the Years

Throughout the years, how restaurant owners communicate with their customers has continued to evolve. Operators want placing an order to be as easy and convenient as possible. Here's a look at how this process has evolved through the years.

1900s–1930s: Ordering was done entirely in person in a facility or drive-in.

1940s: Electronic carhops began taking orders, and early drive-thrus began to appear.

1950s–1960s: Customers could call their favorite restaurants and place their orders, especially for pizza.

1980s: Fax that order in!

1990s–present: Online ordering, ordering by fax machine, and ordering by cell phone. These methods may soon be joined by texting.

period. Some of them decided to make soft drinks. Congress did allow beer drinkers to make "near beer." Near beer's alcoholic content was not to exceed one half of one percent. It tasted terrible, but patrons drank it (and the illegal brews) until the repeal of Prohibition. Amateur beer makers thrived during Prohibition, as did malt and hop shops in the country. There were nearly 100,000 of them throughout the United States, as well as 25,000 stores selling brewing apparatuses.

Hard liquor was also a popular drink in taverns throughout America's early days and through Prohibition. The first distillery opened in Boston as early as 1657 and by the early 1800s there were nearly 2,000 distilleries across the country. Prohibition had a devastating effect on these distilleries. Even though it was a healthy industry prior to Prohibition, most distilleries lacked the resources to make it through these years without sales. Bootleg whiskey was the drink of the hour. When Prohibition was repealed, only about half of the distilleries were able to reopen.

Instead of reducing crime, Prohibition had the opposite effect on the country, and more crime and violence spread across the country as a result of illegal liquor production. Americans had decided Prohibition was not working, even though the government was reluctant to act. By 1933, however, Prohibition was finally repealed.

The National Restaurant Association was formed in 1919 when a group of concerned restaurateurs met in Kansas City, Missouri, over Prohibition. Prohibition did impact restaurants. Their dependence on alcohol sales hurt business and many did go bankrupt. In their place speakeasies sprouted up across the nation, including The 21 Club in New York and the Coconut Grove in Los Angeles.

Despite the negative impact of Prohibition on the restaurant industry, the 1920s and 1930s were a time of tremendous growth for restaurants. Restaurants were no longer considered a luxury—they had become a necessity. The repeal of Prohibition brought the return of beer and alcohol to menus; this helped boost the development of fine-dining and deluxe supper clubs that featured entertainment, like Trader Vic's, Romanoff's, El Morocco, and the Pump Room.

The Rise of Fast-food

The rise of the automobile also had a huge impact on the food services industry. Almost as soon as automobiles hit the road, drive-in restaurants appeared on the scene, ready to quench the thirst and feed the hunger of road weary travelers. Drive-ins were the forerunners of today's fast service segment, serving very similar customers, with the same goal: good food, good service, low price, and all happening speedily. Over the decades they slowly evolved into the fast-food restaurants of today.

The first drive-in restaurant, the Pig Stand, was opened by J. G. Kirby on the Dallas-Fort Worth Highway in 1921. Waitresses ran out to the cars to wait on customers and had to hop up on their running boards to reach them. They soon became known as carhops. However Kirby's somewhat questionably named restaurant was not the first to provide "curbside" food service to customers. Sixteen years earlier, in Memphis, Harold Fortune's drugstore and soda fountain was overrun with customers. It was a hot summer evening, and the number of customers demanding ice cream was exceeding space in the store. Fortune began allowing the gentlemen customers to purchase their ice cream orders and take them outside to their ladies. It was such a success he began offering outdoor service on a regular basis. When automobiles became popular Fortune moved his business to a location that could serve customers in their cars. His restaurant actually created a traffic jam when cars lined the streets waiting for service.

Many of America's most successful and long-standing fast-food restaurants were created during this period. In 1921 Billy Ingram and Walter Anderson started White Castle restaurants with an investment of $700. Their concept was simple. They sold bite-sized burgers for a nickel each. Ingram pioneered many fast-food standards that are important to the success of today's chains, including strict product consistency, unit cleanliness, coupon discounts, heat-resistant cartons for carry-out orders, and folding paper napkins.

Just a few years later, in the summer of 1923, root beer stand owner Roy A. Allen and a former employee Frank Wright opened their first A&W Restaurant near Sacramento, California. In 1925 Howard Dearing Johnson of Wollaston, Massachusetts, took a bankrupt pharmacy and converted it into a soda fountain. When Howard Johnson's first opened it sold three ice cream flavors, vanilla, chocolate, and strawberry, all developed by the proud owner. The soda fountain was a success, so Johnson added a few more items to the menu: hamburgers and hotdogs. Then he opened more units, and lacking capital, he decided to franchise the restaurants. By 1940, Howard Johnson had created 100 franchises and developed 28 ice cream flavors. The Howard Johnson restaurants are credited with being the first to set up franchising.

In Washington, D.C., J. Willard Marriott had an astute observation one hot, sunny, July afternoon in 1927. No one had anywhere to stop for a cold drink. So Marriott put up $3,000 and started his A&W Root Beer store (a franchise operation) with his future wife, Alice. The nine-seat store grossed $16,000 the first year. That was the beginning of the Marriott Corporation. Marriott then developed his own restaurants called Hot Shoppes and developed 20 locations for them spread out from Philadelphia into Florida. He opened his first motel in 1957. At the time of Marriott's death in 1985, the Marriott Corp. owned 1,400 restaurants and 143 hotels and resorts worldwide.

By the end of the 1930s the hamburger was definitely the star item of most restaurants' menus; no menu was considered complete without one. In 1937 the cheeseburger was invented by an entrepreneur named Lionel Sternberger of Glendale, California. Sternberger had purchased the Hinky Dink Barbecue Stand, renaming it the Boulevard Stop. Sternberger planned to serve hamburgers, but he knew that if he was going to compete with the other diners and restaurants in the area his burgers had to be unique. So he started adding sauces, relish, lettuce, and cheese to them. He called it "the aristocratic hamburger with cheese." People loved it. It was almost like getting a complete meal on a bun.

Another burger joint that got its start at this time was Big Boy. When 19-year-old Bob Wian learned a neighbor's six-stool lunch counter was for sale he sold his car and used the money to purchase it. He had started out working at different places as a dishwasher and a fry cook and the restaurant industry was in his blood. A 90-pound six-year-old named Richard Woodruff began hanging out at Bob's counter. Wian gave him odd jobs to do and paid him with food, nicknaming him "Big Boy." Around the same time Wian's friends who played in the Chuck Foster Band would drop over to Wian's to catch a bite to eat after playing. One of them complained about the lack of variety on the menu saying, "Hamburgers! Don't you have anything different?" Wian accepted this culinary challenge and immediately cut a sesame bun into three slices, added two hamburger patties, cheese, lettuce, mayonnaise, and a special relish and handed it to him. Everybody loved and wanted this special burger. Another friend of Wian's was an animation artist. He drew Woodruff in his checkerboard pants, eating a burger. The Big Boy and the Bob's Big Boy Burger became Wian's trademarks.

Ice cream was also undergoing some changes in the 1920s and 1930s. Earlier in the century the ice cream cone had been invented, and by 1924, Americans were eating 245 million ice cream cones annually. The Good Humor bar arrived on the scene in 1920, bringing with it the concept of ice cream on a stick. Another ice cream favorite, Eskimo Pie, was invented in the 1920s. Christian Nelson owned a shop that sold both ice cream and candy. When a little boy in his store could not decide whether to order an ice cream sandwich or a candy bar, Nelson had the idea for a product that would be a combination of the two. He sold the first chocolate covered ice cream bar with no stick in 1921 under the name of Eskimo Pie, and just one year later the company was selling 1 million Eskimo Pies a day. Popsicles were patented in 1924. And while hand-dipped ice cream was already an American icon, Thomas Carvel invented the first soft serve ice cream machine in 1934. The first Dairy Queen opened in Joliet, Illinois, in 1940.

A final development in the industry that occurred during this time period revolved around parking. As drive-ins and diners proliferated, people parked wherever they pleased. Most days this worked out OK, but since most parking lots were gravel or dirt, they quickly became mud pits after a good rain. By the end of this time period, as more attention was paid to a restaurant's exterior, the same attention was then cast on the parking lot. By the end of the 1930s parking lots became paved and lines marked specific places for patrons to park.

Midcentury: 1940–1980

While White Castle, A&W, and Howard Johnsons continued to thrive through the middle of the 20th century, a new generation of entrepreneurs was also ready to have their day in the sun. One of these was Carl N. Karcher. In 1941, Karcher was working as a bakery deliveryman. He had $15 cash and a Plymouth. He borrowed $311 using his car as collateral and purchased a hot dog cart. He made $14.75 his first day in business. His hot dog business succeeded and eventually evolved into a drive-in barbecue and fast-food operation. His menu featured hamburgers and chicken sandwiches. Called Carl Jr.'s, his restaurant spawned other locations and 50 years later he had more than 600 units and made $640 million in sales. Karcher was the first to add several amenities to his restaurants that are standard in today's industry: air conditioning, carpeting, background music, automatic charbroilers, salad bars, nutritional guides, and all-you-can drink beverage bars.

While Karcher was starting Carl Jr.'s, two brothers in San Bernardino, Mo and Dick McDonald, were bucking industry standards and creating their own unique concept in 1940. They opened a 600-square-foot facility that violated a basic rule of kitchen design: it exposed the entire kitchen to customers. Their 25-item menu generated $200,000 in annual sales. Twenty carhops served a huge

On the Cutting Edge

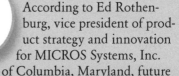

According to Ed Rothenburg, vice president of product strategy and innovation for MICROS Systems, Inc. of Columbia, Maryland, future point of sale (POS) technology will include what he calls the digital wallet. Using SmartPhones and similar technologies, customers will be able to connect directly to a restaurant's POS system and place and pay for their orders.

parking lot designed to hold 125 cars full of hungry customers. But competition for the drive-in dollar was fierce in the 1940s, so feeling the pressure of competition and the strain of maintaining a large staff of carhops, the McDonald brothers made some drastic changes to their business model. In 1948 they eliminated carhops, closed the restaurant, and converted the service line to walk-up windows. They also lowered the price of the hamburgers from $.30 each to $.15 each, cut their menu to 10 items, and created a production line to efficiently and quickly produce the food. In another daring move to save costs McDonald's did away with plates and silverware —after all, hamburgers and fries are finger foods. Speedy service was their goal and they boasted that they could "bag" a customer's meal in 20 seconds. It took a few months for customers to adjust, but the changes were a financial success. Annual sales jumped to $300,000, and franchising soon followed. The infamous golden arches arrived on the scene at the Phoenix, Arizona, location in 1953. By 1961 McDonald's had sold 500 million hamburgers.

In the 1950s new entrepreneurs and existing operators were noticing the McDonald brothers' success. Similar concepts began opening across the country. With names like Pay-Tak, Thrift-O-Mat, Hamburger Hand-Out, and the Cheese Hut, obviously none of these achieved the same level of success as the restaurant they copied— with one exception. In Florida, Burger King opened with some innovative ideas. They offered $.18 burgers and "Insta" machines that made malts and burgers. However the big name "fast-food" chain operators of the 1950s were still mostly drive-in concepts: Bob's Big Boy, Steak 'N Shake, Sonic, Dog 'N Suds, and A&W.

Midcentury Dining Trends

During the 1940s Americans began looking at restaurants in a different way. They were not just a place to go as a special treat anymore; they were becoming an important part of our daily lives. In 1941 there were more than 150,000 eating places in America with a total seating capacity of 11.6 million. Twelve million meals were served at restaurants that year. But as the McDonald brothers experienced firsthand, the 1940s were also a challenging time for food service operators when it came to staffing. World War II drained the nation's men from the workforce, and many women stepped up to take their places. They worked primarily in factories, leaving teenagers as the primary pool of workers for the food services industry. Operators found teens unreliable and struggled to maintain a high level of service quality. After the war ended it took a few years for restaurants to recover. Returning soldiers initially looked for higher paying work than that offered at restaurants. Owners still hired young, inexperienced workers to keep their restaurants staffed. They developed training programs, and to attract more seasoned staff members, also began offering profit sharing and other benefits. These efforts paid off and eventually service quality returned.

By the 1950s the industry was again tackling a problem related to teens, especially drive-in restaurants. Soda fountains had been the place for teens to hang out in the 1930s and early 1940s, but by the end of the 1940s teens had switched their loyalties to drive-in restaurants. Soda fountains had been converting to the more lucrative drive-in model, so teens followed. Depending on the group of teens that chose your locale this could be a blessing or a curse. At the least it was a nuisance for most operators. Teens arrived early and did not leave until closing. They made meals out of fries and a shake and took up space other hungry customers could have used. In addition, teens' behavior ranged from challenging to outright acts of vandalism. Stolen silverware, initials carved into booths, slashed upholstery, and jammed juke boxes were commonplace in drive-ins across the country.

Drive-ins were a leading segment in the industry through the 1940s, and there was a wide range of food served in them. One item, the hamburger, almost seemed like a prerequisite, but many offered choices that ranged from smoked salmon to jellied chicken loaf with fruit salad (not the most appetizing sounding dish). But operators learned over the years that trying to maintain inventory for a big menu of items was cost-prohibitive and eliminated many items in favor of those that were tried and true.

They also began making changes, trying to create a competitive edge and reduce costs like McDonald's. Operators were looking for options to reduce personnel, specifically carhops. This need in addition to customers' growing desire for speedy service led to many innovations and changes. One restaurant designed a conveyer belt that delivered customers' food in cardboard boxes to their cars. More practical ideas occurred in the late 1940s with the idea of take-out and take-home food. Many drive-ins already offered this option, but by the end of the decade many were considering it as the only dining option.

By the 1950s, eating out was a $16 billion a year industry, according to the National Restaurant Association. This growing trend in eating out was attributed to a larger population, shorter workweek, people traveling more, and a greater demand for take-home food. Teenagers were not the only age demographic that enjoyed eating at drive-ins. In the 1950s families began eating there more often, and operators did all they could to cultivate their business. This was when family-friendly restaurant innovations like "kiddie-size" portions and "junior menus" evolved. Restaurants offered kids' birthday packages and gave treats or prizes to kids at the end of the meal.

But teens were still creating a problem for drive-in owners. They kept families away, littering the parking lots and raising the volume on their car radios to a blare that was uncomfortable for families. Operators used several tactics to try to appease both the teens and families, but because of the loss of families they were quickly losing money. Restaurant owners tried placing minimum order quantities or time limits. Some created a gate and token system, while others even hired guards and created teen disturbance policies. But none of them worked. The teens became even more unruly, bucking the efforts to rein them in, and neighbors complained that the kids yelled out "indecent" language and threw beer cans and bottles in the streets.

There were two restaurants during the 1950s that were the first to create drive-thru operations. One was in Billings, Montana, a restaurant called Big Boy (which was not affiliated with Bob's Big Boy). The other was called the Tastee In and Out in Lincoln, Nebraska. Each installed microphones along the driveways leading to their facilities. After using the microphone to order their meals, customers drove the short distance to the building and picked them up.

Microphones were not the only electronic devices designed and considered to help boost the dwindling market of drive-ins. One invention created to save on labor costs was the electronic carhop. This device consisted of a speaker, microphone, and serving station equipped with a permanent menu and tray table. Customers pushed one button and were connected to an operator who took their food orders. Then if they chose, they could push another button and listen to music until a carhop arrived to deliver the order and their bill.

By the end of the 1950s new menu items were also popping up all over the country. Some of them were so popular they spawned their own restaurants. The ever-growing restaurant market was now flooded with pancake houses, donut shops, steak houses, and

INTERVIEW

Trends of the Industry

Bruce Grindy
Senior economist with the National Restaurant Association in Washington, D.C.

When examining the food service industry's history one fact becomes crystal clear: successful operations adapt and change to meet customer's needs. As people's lives became busier, the need for ready-prepared foods created a growing demand. Concepts that adapted to meeting that demand have become leaders in their markets. We asked industry veteran Bruce Grindy about the industry's history and its impact on the future.

How can looking at the history of the industry help us identify trends, both positive and negative?
The overarching historical trend of the industry has been the evolution from luxury to necessity. This will continue into the future, as operators continue to find ways to provide convenient options for their customers.

How can it prevent future mistakes?
Continue to evolve and respond to customer wants and needs. If we look at industries that are struggling today, it is often those that do not adapt to meet the changing times.

How has the industry's past shaped its current status?
A hallmark of the industry has been its ability to continually adapt to meet the ever-changing wants and needs of the dining public. And this will continue well into the future. Customers twenty years from now will have options we cannot even think of today, just as we have options that customers twenty years ago would never have dreamed of.

increasingly popular pizza parlors. And like all other good ideas in the industry, pizza shops began to franchise. The early franchises in the 1950s were Pizza Hut, Domino's, and Little Caesar's.

Another segment that gained momentum in the 1950s was coffee shops. These restaurants were known primarily for their hearty breakfasts. Two examples of these that quickly became chain operations were Denny's and IHOP.

The 1960s became the decade known for innovative marketing concepts. Drive-ins were slowly becoming a thing of the past, yesterday's idea, as one by one they converted to different, more stable and lucrative models, like take-home, self-service, or fast-food operations. Successful full-service concepts that began in the 1960s include TGI Fridays, Arby's, Subway, Steak & Ale, Red Lobster, and Wendy's. Large fast-food chains became public companies in the 1960s, including Kentucky Fried Chicken and Denny's.

By the end of 1969 more fast-food entrepreneurs wanted their turn at bat, opening new stores in the hopes of matching the success of restaurants that were now giants in the segment, like McDonald's. Two of these include Columbus, Ohio's Dave Thomas. A former Kentucky Fried Chicken franchisee, Thomas named his square hamburger restaurant after his daughter Wendy. And in Lexington, Kentucky—nowhere near an ocean—the first Long John Silver's Fish & Chips opened its doors.

Television was beginning to have an impact on the food service industry as early as the 1960s. Televised cooking shows increased consumer awareness of what constituted good food. In 1966, chef and author Julia Child, considered a pioneer in television cooking, received an Emmy for her show *The French Chef.* Child had started her career in the 1930s as an advertising copywriter. It was not until after her marriage to Paul Child in 1946 that Child was introduced to French cuisine. Child was employed by the United States Foreign Service and the couple moved to Paris in 1948. Child was delighted by French cuisine and studied at the Cordon Bleu school, then under two French chefs. Her passion for French cuisine led her to help with the writing of *Mastering the Art of French Cooking*, which was published in 1961. The impact of the book was to inspire home cooks everywhere to expand their cooking skills. Child was much beloved by her readers and television audiences, and created a much wider interest in cooking and fine-dining.

Customers continued to crave the new and different. In 1967 McDonald's decided to satisfy that craving as it test marketed a double-decker burger called the Big Mac. They rolled out the Big Mac nationwide the following year. Food processors and suppliers also began looking at their customers as potential partners. In 1967 Pillsbury purchased Burger King's 274 units for $18 million, and in 1968 General Mills purchased the 1,000-unit Burger Chef for $20 million. That same year Ralston Purina acquired controlling interest in Foodmaker, the parent company of Jack in the Box.

The late 1960s were also years when food manufacturers sought to satisfy consumers' cravings for new and different foods. In 1969 two fabricated potato chips were introduced, Proctor & Gamble's Pringles, and another version called Chipos, put on the market by General Mills. This was also the year Kellogg's introduced Frosted Mini-Wheats cereal.

In many homes both parents worked, meaning they had less time for household duties like cooking. But it also meant there was more disposable income available. Busy working parents were looking for convenience at home, on the job, and in leisure activities, including restaurants. On the home front Pepsi Co. sought to oblige, introducing the first two-liter bottle of Pepsi in 1970. General Mills came up with Hamburger Helper, and Orville Redenbacher and his partner Charles Bowman introduced their gourmet popcorn to an increasingly discerning generation of consumers.

By the 1970s restaurants were a $42.8 billion industry. Televised cooking shows continued to gain popularity, affecting consumers' attitudes and choices when they chose to eat out, which they were continuing to do with ever-increasing regularity. Like the expansion of menus in the late 1950s, the 1970s saw even more expansion, as ethnic foods such as Chinese, Mexican, and Indian cuisines began a dramatic rise in popularity. By the 1970s women had entered the workforce in larger numbers, and they began entering food service management and executive positions. According to the Women's FoodService Forum, by this time 14 women held executive positions at large companies, and formed this association so that others would have an easier time achieving this level of success. Today the Forum has more than 3,700 members.

By the end of the 1970s food service professionals were beginning to see customer interest in healthier foods, vegetarian menu items, and the beginning of "California cuisine." Wendy's was one of the first fast-food restaurants to recognize the need for healthier fare when it offered a salad bar in 1979. New restaurants that opened in the 1970s tended to be theme-oriented, like Hard Rock Café, which opened its first location in London in 1971, and Chili's Grill and Bar, which opened in Dallas in 1975.

Another trend in restaurants in the 1970s was to create new menu items in an effort to keep customers interested or lure new ones in the door. McDonald's launched two new menu items in the 1970s, the Egg McMuffin, and in an effort to compete with Wendy's, the Quarter Pounder. Denny's introduced the Grand Slam Breakfast in 1977, while Arby's offered its new Beef 'n Cheddar sandwich in 1978. This was also the decade that launched the current-day coffee house craze, with the first Starbucks opening in Seattle, Washington, in 1971.

The 1980s were challenging years for most food service operators. The economy was in bad shape and restaurants were hard hit by the downturn of the recession in the '80s. There was turmoil in the industry and the result was, according to West & Wood's *Introduction to Foodservice*, ". . . unbridled expansion, overleveraged buyouts, employee buyouts, operators filing for Chapter 11, system-wide restructuring, downsizing, and job layoffs."

New United States' legislation was proposed and enacted to improve the environment. The new legislation along with solid waste proposals and health and nutrition mandates all impacted operators' costs. As a result, major mergers and acquisitions between restaurants and food processors and manufacturers began to occur around 1982 and picked up momentum throughout the decade. In 1982, Hardee's acquired the 650-unit Burger Chef from General Foods, converting many of the Burger Chef units to Hardee's. H.J. Heinz Co. acquired two businesses in 1984: Borden's $225 million food service business, and the $200 million All American Gourmet. Also in 1984 Consolidated Foods, which later became Sara Lee, acquired Jimmy Dean meats. The year 1985 also proved eventful for the industry. R.J. Reynolds acquired Nabisco Brands for $4.6 billion and changed its name to RJR Nabisco. In the same year Marriott Corporation acquired the Howard Johnson restaurant and motel chain. It sold most of the hotels and converted many of the restaurants into Big Boy units the following year. In 1987 International Dairy Queen acquired Orange Julius. By 1988 the consolidation trend intensified and it was a huge year for mergers and acquisitions in the industry. Grand Metropolitan plc, a British conglomerate, paid $5.79 billion to acquire Pillsbury, along with its Häagen-Dazs ice cream division and Burger King restaurants. In the same year Phillip Morris bought Kraft Foods for $13.1 billion and added it to their General Foods division. They renamed the combined entity Kraft General Foods and it became the largest food company in the world. Also in 1988 SYSCO acquired CFS Continental to become the largest food service distributor in North America, and Hershey Foods sold its Friendly's Ice Cream restaurant chain to Chicago-based Tennessee Restaurant Co. Tennessee Restaurant already owned 330 Perkins locations. And rounding out the decade of consolidation, Allied-Lyons acquired the

2,000-unit Dunkin' Donuts chain in 1989. The result was increased competition for business for independent restaurant owners, and consumers saw fewer independent restaurants and more chains throughout this time period.

The tough economic times did not deter restaurant entrepreneurs from opening new restaurants during the decade. Examples of restaurants that launched during the 1980s include: Wolfgang Puck's restaurant, Spago, which opened in Los Angeles in 1982; that same year General Mills opened its first Olive Garden restaurant; Culver's Frozen Custard Butterburgers opened in Wisconsin in 1984; and the first Boston Chicken restaurant opened in Newton, Massachusetts, in 1985. But no significant restaurant openings occurred during the last half of the decade.

The healthier-foods trend that started in the 1970s continued into the 1980s. Kellogg's introduced Nutri-Grain whole grain cereals in 1981; Diet Coke was launched in 1982; Wendy's added baked potatoes to its menu in 1983; in 1990 McDonald's and Burger King stopped frying their foods in beef fat and released ingredient information to the public; in 1989 ConAgra launched ten Healthy Choice dinners, designed to be low-calorie, low-salt, low-fat, and low-cholesterol. The Healthy Choice brand has expanded and is still successful today.

Many chain restaurants that did not consolidate or take other measures to maintain their revenues during the 1980s closed. Restaurants that did not survive the 1980s include Flakey Jake's and D-Lites of America.

The 1990s to the Present

Most of the trends that started in the 1970s and 1980s continued to play a role in how food service operators did business in the 1990s. Mergers and buyouts of both restaurants and food companies continued to occur throughout the 1990s. This time some of the buyouts occurred to spread company risk to different markets. One example is McDonald's acquisition of the Chipotle Mexican Grill concept in 1998. If one large chain was not merging with another, it was filing its initial public offering (IPO) and selling stock. Included in the list of restaurants that filed IPOs in the 1990s are Au Bon Pain, IHOP, Sonic, and Outback Steakhouse. Restaurants and food manufacturers continued to produce and market healthier options for their customers, although some merely tried to create a healthier image. For example Kentucky Fried Chicken changed its name to KFC so customers would not think of it as a fried food restaurant.

Ethnic foods' popularity increased throughout these years—in fact, by 1991 salsa began to outsell ketchup in retail stores. Brave entrepreneurs continued to launch new restaurant concepts in a saturated, competitive market. One concept that launched in the 1990s was Planet Hollywood. In 1996 it launched the Official All-Star Café in New York's Time Square and completed an initial public offering, raising $190 million, setting a record for the most actively-traded IPO in NASDAQ history.

Co-branding was another new trend that began in the late 1990s and has gained popularity ever since. Co-branding refers to the business model in which two different restaurant concepts owned by the same parent company are housed together under one roof; examples include many Taco Bell/Pizza Hut combinations and Long John Silver's/A&W. YUM Brands, owner of these concepts, began incorporating the co-branding model to give consumers more choices when visiting an establishment. No other company has used this strategy as extensively, or achieved its level of success.

Another restaurant marketing concept that began in the 1990s that has gained popularity is placing restaurants (either full-size menu or a scaled-back version) in retail stores, discount stores, gas stations, and other locations, rather than building standalone facilities. For example, Little Caesar's contracted with K-Mart to open restaurants in 400 of their stores in 1991. Since this partnership began more K-Marts have incorporated the restaurants into their stores and new stores typically contain the restaurants.

Still, many operators, both large and small, went out of business or filed bankruptcy during these years due to changes in the economy and increased consolidations. A few victims of the 1990s were Service America, the $1 billion noncommercial food service operation, and Western Sizzlin, the 350-unit budget steakhouse. Both filed for Chapter 11 in 1992.

New trends that occurred during this decade and beyond relate to consumers' increasing use of technology, starting with cell phones. In the late 1990s some restaurants reacted to cell phones' newfound ubiquity by posting rules or banning their use entirely. Since then the prevalence of cell phones has created the need to revise these policies.

By the late 1990s the increased usage of the Internet began affecting restaurant operations. Large operators began to recognize the value of marketing on the Internet and ordering food using fax machines, cell phones, and online ordering systems, as technology continued to make life busier for families. "The Internet grew exponentially in acceptance [by operators and customers] for getting an order for carry-out or delivery," says Ed Rothenburg, vice president of product strategy and innovation for MICROS Systems, Inc. of Columbia, Maryland. MICROS supplies enterprise applications for the hospitality industry. "More and more people are placing orders and picking them up [using cell phones or the Internet]." Rothenburg predicts that soon customers will be able to text message their orders and payment information to restaurants. Rothenburg says that the new generation emerging from colleges and universities prefers communicating in that form, and it is all about managing customer relationships.

Throughout the years the bottom line has been to meet customers' needs and do it a little differently than the next operator. The industry's colorful and fascinating history shows that food service is a place where creativity shines through.

A Brief Chronology

1642: The first tavern is opened in America by William Kieft, governor of New Amsterdam.

1750: Thomas Lepper opens his tavern, called The Leopard.

1801: Thomas Jefferson, the third president of the United States, brings French cuisine to the White House and his estate Monticello.

1831: The first fine-dining restaurant in the United States, Delmonico's, launches in New York.

1888: Cocoa-Cola hits the market.

1903: Georges Escoffier publishes his groundbreaking book on French cooking techniques and kitchen organization, *Le Guide Culinaire*.

1919: Prohibition is enacted in 1919, affecting the California wine industry and restaurants everywhere. The National Restaurant Association is created when a group of restaurateurs meet to discuss Prohibition's impact.

1921: Drive-in restaurants, the forerunner of fast-food restaurants, are created in response to drivers' dining needs. The first drive-in, The Pig Stand, opens in 1921. White Castle also opens in 1921.

1933: Prohibition is repealed.

1937: The cheeseburger is invented by Lionel Sternberger of Glendale, California.

1940: The first Dairy Queen opens in Joliet, Illinois.

1941: Carl Jr.'s restaurants launched in 1941. McDonald's began operating in the 1940s.

1941: By this year there were more than 150,000 eating places in America with a total seating capacity of 11.6 million.

1953: The infamous golden arches of McDonald's are first used in the company's building design at its location in Phoenix, Arizona.

1961: By this year McDonald's had sold more than 500 million hamburgers.

1966: Chef and author Julia Child receives an Emmy for her television show *The French Chef.*

1967: McDonald's launches the Big Mac.

1969: The first Wendy's opens in Columbus, Ohio.

1971: The Hard Rock Café opens its first location in London.

1975: Chili's Grill and Bar opens in Dallas.

1977: Denny's introduces the Grand Slam Breakfast.

1982: Wolfgang Puck opens Spago in Los Angeles.

1983: Wendy's offers baked potatoes at all of its locations.

1991: Salsa outsells ketchup at retail stores.

1996: Planet Hollywood launches in New York.

Late '90s to present: Increased use of Internet and technology to place and pay for food orders for take out.

Chapter 2

State of the Industry

"You Gotta Eat, Right?" Who has not heard that question at least once? One of the biggest factors in the food services industry's favor is that eating is truly a necessity of life. More people than ever before view *eating out* as part of that necessity. In fact, according to the National Restaurant Association's 2009 Industry Forecast, 45 percent of adults say restaurants are an essential part of their lifestyles, 1 in 3 say they are not eating out as often as they wish, and 35 percent of adults say that on a weekly basis they are not purchasing take-out foods or having restaurant food delivered as often as they would like, primarily because of concerns about the economy.

Despite the fact that Americans are still concerned about financial security and are tightening their pocketbooks, the National Restaurant Association says that restaurant sales will continue to grow this year, to a record $566 billion. True, they will not grow at the rate the industry has seen in the last several years, but growth is still growth. This could be attributed to the continuing demand for convenience by families on the go. Edna Morris, an industry veteran of more than 30 years, has served in executive capacities with Hardee's and Qunicy's Steakhouse. She is currently the CEO of Genshai Ollin and developing a restaurant concept around locally grown food. She says the industry remains very vibrant even in tough times. "People may be going out to eat fewer times, or not ordering a bottle of wine, but they are still going out," she says. Morris says the status of the restaurant industry is often a leading indicator of the economy in general. "When there is discretionary money to go out sales go up,"

Morris says. "The restaurant industry is the first to be affected by a rough economy but it is also the first to emerge."

However, Technomic, a research-based food services consulting firm, also offers a forecast and it is not as rosy as the NRA's. Technomic predicts sales in 2009 will decline by 2.2 percent. Most segments will decline or hold their own, and the largest jump in sales will be in the educational food services sector, which Technomic predicts will increase by a modest 3 percent.

Still, the industry is huge, and despite its mammoth size it is surprisingly adaptable, nimbly changing to meet ever-changing customer needs. Currently more than 945,000 restaurants compete in the United States and employ 13 million people. And that does not include food service suppliers, which is itself a $38 billion industry.

Its adaptability is just what allows it to succeed, say many industry veterans. It is critical for operators today to know their customers' needs, and supply them. Most people in the industry recognize that the two top needs consumers have today are for convenience and fast service. According to *The Food Service Industry: Trends and Changing Structure in the New Millennium* by Charlotte G. Friddle, Sandeep Mangaraj, and Jean D. Kinsey, time and convenience are essentials of today's and tomorrow's lifestyles and cooking. Younger generations are relying more heavily on ready-prepared foods from grocery stores and restaurants and are spending less time in the kitchen.

In addition, providing good service and quality food are as important as making it convenient and quick. "A customer always wants good service appropriate to the concept—fine-dining, fast casual, or fast-food," says Donatos Pizza Founder and CEO Jim Grote. "The customer may put up with 'poor' service to get a good price and a quality product when money is scarce, but they will remember who gave the best service and took care of them when times are better."

The Challenges Ahead

According to the National Restaurant Association, operators across all segments cite rising costs as their number one challenge in the coming 2009–2010. Food and energy costs continue to rise, and since customers' budgets are still tight, raising prices is not necessarily the answer. Most restaurant managers say they plan to cover rising costs by increasing sales. The best way to do this, they say, is to focus on repeat business. They plan to reward repeat customers with discounts, and listen to their needs, especially in the quick service

Everyone ....▶
Knows

Organic versus Healthful

One of the hottest trends in the food service industry is the increased demand for organic and healthy foods. But what many in the food service industry do not know is that *organic* does not equal *healthful*. The United States Food and Drug Administration dictates what foods can be labeled organic and what can be labeled healthful. "Organic" refers to a product that has been produced without manmade chemicals of any kind. The end product can still be high in fat, sugar, sodium, and calories—hardly healthful! Only foods that meet the FDA's guidelines in fat, sugar, sodium, and calories are allowed to be labeled "healthful."

category. Repeat customers account for 75 percent of sales at quick service restaurants, according to the National Restaurant Association's quick service operator survey, so retaining these valuable customers will be a priority in the coming years.

Other challenges restaurants face in the current economic environment are battling the competition, and obtaining financing. As banks and other financial institutions tighten the reins on loans, operators have found it harder to get credit than in years past. Smart operators are renegotiating lease terms, carefully studying their cash flow, carefully planning, and reducing costs wherever possible to counter the reduced availability of financing.

Employment, Wages, and Profit

Recruiting, hiring, and retaining quality workers have long been the bane of operators' existence. In fact hiring and retaining employees usually tops the lists of food service operators' challenges. In 2009 the story was a bit different. Because of the rise in unemployment, restaurateurs and food service operations were able to meet their employment needs. But this will not be a continuing trend. The restaurant industry's inherent turnover rates (due to young team members) means it is continually hiring.

The food services industry—especially the restaurant industry, which constitutes well over half of the industry—is one of the largest employers in the United States. Restaurants alone represent 9 percent of the nation's total job base, according to the National Restaurant Association. In 2008 the industry expanded its workforce by 1.6 percent. But in January of 2009, according to the United States Bureau of Labor Statistics, employment in the leisure and hospitality industry had dropped from 13.5 million to 13.3 million, a 1.5 percent drop, and this trend continued through the first quarter of 2009, with the number employed in the industry dropping to 13.2 million by the end of the quarter, an additional .8 percent drop.

The good news for employees, however, is that the average hourly wage for production employees in the leisure and hospitality industry continues to increase. In the last ten years the average hourly wage rose by more than $2 an hour from $8.13 per hour in December of 1999 to $10.94 per hour by December of 2008, according to the United States Bureau of Labor Statistics. This may not be so good for managers and operators trying to control costs. But a higher hourly wage will attract more people to fill jobs, which, as mentioned before, are plentiful due to turnover of young employees.

Even though the hourly wage has risen, the average number of hours worked in a week has declined over the last ten years. According to the United States Bureau of Labor Statistics, in December 1999 employees in the commercial food services industry worked an average of 26.1 hours per week. By December 2008, that number had dropped to 25.0.

The current rise in unemployment has actually helped meet labor shortages in the food services industry, but the National Restaurant Association is predicting that 2009 will be the first year since 1991 the industry will actually cut jobs overall, rather than increase its employment base, and so far U.S. Bureau of Labor Statistics are backing up that projection. The National Restaurant Association is also predicting, however, a significant increase in its workforce over the next 10 years. In its 2009 Industry Forecast the association predicts that by 2019 the restaurant industry will employ 14.8 million people, an increase of 14 percent. The labor force during this same time period is only expected to grow by 9 percent, creating a shortage of workers in the industry. The association also predicts that three states in the country will experience the fastest growth in jobs: Texas, Nevada, and Florida, because of growing populations in these states.

The demographics of this workforce may see a definite change. Many operators depend on younger workers for the bulk of their labor needs. In fact 50 percent of workers in the industry today are under age 25, but statistics show that fewer people in this age group are entering the workforce. According to the association, 59 percent of 16- to 24-year-olds were in the labor force in 2008, a drop of nearly 10 percentage points over the last 20 years.

On the other end of the demographic spectrum, more baby boomers and older adults are retiring and looking for ways to supplement their incomes. The number of Americans age 65 or older that are working continues to rise, and it may be from this pool that food service operators need to draw. Adults age 65 and older reached a labor-force participation rate of 16.7 percent in 2008, nearly a 40-year high, and the number of individuals age 65 or older in the workforce is expected to grow 80 percent in the next decade!

As an up and coming employee of the industry, you may be wondering where most of this growth is going to occur over the next 10 years. The National Restaurant Association predicts that by 2019 there will be an additional 40,000 food service managers on the job, an increase of 14.1 percent. Jobs that will experience the highest growth by 2019 are fast-food preparers and counter workers (an increase of 16.1 percent), food preparation workers (an increase of 16.0 percent), and chefs and head cooks (15.8 percent).

As the need for labor rises, as well as the costs of hiring, operators will be looking at other options in terms of getting things done. The National Restaurant Association's forecast says most operators plan to improve their restaurants' productivity to decrease the need for workers. That is not the only option, however. Jim Grote, founder and CEO of Donatos Pizza, says centralized locations for food preparation may become more prevalent.

Current Trends

Any trend in the food services industry is geared toward meeting a particular customer need, whether that is for faster service, added convenience, or healthier menu choices. Many of the trends spreading throughout the industry today started during the 1970s, when a growing number of two-parent working families wanted an easier way to feed their families. These parents and their children were often on the go, but parents were worried they were sacrificing the health of their children for the convenience of fast-food. In response, healthier menu items, especially for children, began to appear at restaurants as early as the late 1970s.

Edna Morris, an industry veteran and CEO of Genshai Ollin, says that healthful food choices will definitely continue as a trend well into the future. "People want healthful food," Morris says. "They want to know that it is less processed and handled and that the growers are committed to sustainability. People want to understand where their food comes from. You will be seeing more wholesome options and at the same time a consciousness about reducing our carbon footprint. People don't want their food to come from 3,000 miles away. That will continue to shape the industry."

Francine Cohen, editor in chief of *Food and Beverage Magazine*, agrees, adding that more restaurants will be buying fresh foods from local growers. "There's something to be said about going to a farmer's market and getting the best price for the best product," she says. "It's not realistic to expect that chefs will get all their foods locally, but they do as much as they possibly can. It's a very creative thing to do and gives them the possibility to change up their menus."

The National Restaurant Association surveyed more than 1,600 chefs and asked them to rank more than 200 items in terms of how hot a trend they were. These chefs ranked the use of locally grown produce the number one trend in the country, which also relates to the industry's growing desire for "going green."

Another trend that is sweeping the nation, according to the National Restaurant Association survey, is mini-desserts. Restaurants in all categories are recognizing the need for smaller dessert options, and are cashing in on smaller-scale versions of customers' favorites. For example, Mongolian's BD Barbecue is offering mini-desserts based on their larger scale versions. The new desserts satisfy customers' cravings for something sweet, but meet their desire for smaller and less expensive options. On the opposite end of the popularity scale is pie. Although chefs felt pies are perennial favorites, they are the least trendy dessert option out there.

The trends that rank third and fourth in the National Restaurant Industry's survey tie back to the idea of more healthful menu options. The third trend is the use of organic produce, and the fourth is the availability of nutritionally balanced options for children on a growing number of restaurant menus. Victor Gielisse, associate vice president at the Culinary Institute of America in New York City notes this trend, but adds that unless these more healthful options are also

Fast

Facts

10 Jobs Projected to Experience the Most Growth by 2019

1. Fast food preparers and counter workers, up 1.5 percent
2. Food preparation workers, up 1.5 percent
3. Chefs and head cooks, up 1.5 percent
4. Food and beverage serving workers, up 1.4 percent
5. Supervisors, food preparation, and serving workers, up 1.4 percent
6. First-line supervisors/managers of food-preparation and serving workers, up 1.4 percent
7. Counter attendants, cafeteria, food concession, and coffee shop, up 1.4 percent
8. Waiters and waitresses, up 1.4 percent
9. Cooks, restaurant, up 1.3 percent
10. Food servers, non-restaurant, up 1.3 percent

(http://www.restaurant.org)

tasty they may not stay on the menu for long. "There is an emphasis on resources, where the food is coming from," says Gielisse. "And people want healthier foods. Diet and nutrition have to be met, but the first thing that comes to mind is they are tasteless. How can we layer flavor complexities, seasonings, garnishes, in food preparation so food is healthy and flavorful? Food preparation is the key."

New cuts of meat rank fifth in the association's Top Trend list. Examples of these include the Denver steak, pork flat iron, and bone-in Tuscan veal chop. Other trends that chefs cite in the survey include the use of superfruits (mangosteen, açai, and goji berry), fruits and vegetables as side dishes in children's meals, and tapas, or small plate dishes on menus. Tapas first appeared on the scene in Spain, and are served at nearly every establishment there. They are similar to appetizers but they are not eaten as a warm up for more food. They are eaten instead of an entrée and are served with a cocktail. Often people will go to more than one location for a drink and tapas. Tapas allow customers to taste a restaurant's offerings without loading up on food and they provide a less expensive way to explore the menu.

Items that hit bottom in popularity on the survey include French fries and other fried foods, baked potatoes, and potato salad. Keep in mind that this means they are not considered a hot new trend, not that they will be disappearing from menus in the near future. In fact a large number of the chefs surveyed consider these perennial favorites.

Gielisse also notes that many people are looking for authentic food experiences. "People used to say they were looking for ethnic food," he says. "Now they say they want authentic Spanish, or French." Gielisse says this trend can be attributed to the proliferation of television shows. "People are more educated when it comes to food now."

Menu items aside, there are other trends that will continue to grow in 2009. Convenience is at the top of that list. "Convenience is always a huge trend and important to consumers," Morris notes. "People want to be seated when they are ready. They are time-starved, time-crunched, and want food when it works for them. Operators who can meet that need will be rewarded handsomely."

Technology will play a more dominant role in restaurant operations in the future. Long hours are historically part and parcel with the food services industry. No matter how successful a restaurant is, or how excellent the staff members, the business requires the owner to be present to stay on top of day-to-day operations. But enhanced point of sale (POS) systems are paving the way to better working hours for today's entrepreneurs, according to Ed Rothenberg, vice president of product strategy and innovation at MICROS Systems, Inc. Rothenberg says new systems will alert owners when too many "no sales" are rung up at the cash register, or there is a scheduling problem. "You can immediately and remotely manage the business," says Rothenberg. Technology will also impact how operators manage customer relationships, and how customers can order and receive their food.

So which segments of the industry are most likely to succeed in the future? According to the National Restaurant Association projections, the only segment in the commercial side of the industry that will not experience a downturn in sales over the next year will be limited or quick service restaurants. This segment will achieve a very small growth rate of .4 percent in 2009. While remaining segments will see decreases in sales, the segment least affected will be bars and taverns. Evidently Americans can cut back on eating out when times are tough, but cutting back on visits to their favorite watering holes is not a part of the plan. Bars and taverns are projected to see a .4 percent decrease in sales in 2009. Other segments that will see more modest downturns in sales are social caterers at -1.6 percent and full-service restaurants at -2.5 percent. The segment projected to experience the steepest drop in sales is cafeterias, grill-buffets, and buffets, at -5.2 percent.

Technology

The food services industry has not been immune to the explosion of new technologies that started in the 1990s and has continued to escalate ever since. The combination of computers, POS systems, and the Internet has broadened operators' horizons and abilities to serve and communicate with customers.

As mentioned earlier, improvements to POS technologies have allowed restaurant owners to remotely manage their restaurants. MICROS Systems' Rothenberg says it boils down to enforcing standards. "Let's say I have opened a restaurant," he says. "I have chosen the real estate, created the menu, hired the servers, decorated the interior, and kept the parking lot clean. I'm there 20 hours a day making sure the restaurant is running the way I want it to." In other words, he says, he now has no personal life, and if he wants to open another location how does he ensure both are running according to his standards? Today's POS systems can solve these problems.

"The technology monitors inventory and production," Rothenberg says. "It looks at consistency. In almost every area you can set standards, the system can measure them, create reports, and allow you to see whether they are being met."

There are systems that track inventory, staffing, and scheduling. If an operator is short-staffed during a high-volume daypart the system will send him or her an alert. If a cashier is keying too many "no sales" transactions on the cash register, the manager will receive an alert. "The moment something happens you can immediately be notified and react," Rothenberg says. He also notes that operators can use the alert system for routine tasks, like checking the status of restrooms and the parking lot. Most POS technologies today offer information solutions for both front-of-house and back-of-house operations.

With convenience already high on consumers' priority lists more decision-makers in the hospitality industry are considering self-service kiosks, similar to those currently found in grocery stores and other retail outlets. NCR, a leading technology company based in Dayton, Ohio, says self-service kiosks may be a very important trend in the food service industry. A study conducted by NCR says that consumers are getting increasingly frustrated with long waits at traditional check-out lines at restaurants. According to NCR, one-third of the operators in the hospitality industry have said they are considering the use of this technology. NCR cites economic factors, labor challenges, and customer trends as the reason for the interest in this technology. Still, more than 40 percent of the operators surveyed by NCR are reluctant to start self-service kiosks. Most of these operators cite the upfront cost of installing the kiosks as the leading deterrent, but with rising labor costs, self-service kiosks may begin to look more attractive. NCR is also quick to add that self-service is more than just a kiosk. Other self-service options that are growing in popularity include ordering on the Internet, and ordering via a mobile device, such as a cell phone or a personal digital assistant (PDA). Rothenberg says these options are going to play a bigger role in the industry as college kids enter the workforce. "This [text messaging] is the way they communicate," he says. Digital wallets, where a customer can text his or her order and pay for it, will be the wave of the future.

While all these new technologies may have very positive impacts on an operator's future bottom line, most are still more concerned about today's bottom line and how technology can help them weather the current economic crisis. Participants at the 14th Annual International Foodservice Technology Exposition in Orlando, Florida, held in February of 2009, said their departments were using systems that monitor spending and hardware and software that aid front-of-house operations to help their companies cut costs and drive customer traffic. Most of these participants are chief information officers (CIO) at large chains like Subway and Dunkin' Donuts. Their primary concern is helping their franchisees succeed, and in some cases just survive these tough economic times. The information that can be gathered through current POS systems allows them to do that. Glenn West, senior vice president of information systems and electronic commerce for Papa John's International Inc. in Louisville, Kentucky, says that if a technology cannot yield immediate results for franchisees, it is being deferred until economic conditions improve.

That is not to say other technologies are not being considered by many operators. Among the technologies discussed at the 2009 Orlando Technology Expo, the ones that were deemed most "discussion-worthy" were remote ordering and pay-at-table systems, Payment Card Industry (PCI) compliance and data security, and mobile marketing.

The role of the Internet is definitely increasing in the industry as well, and there are many facets of its use, from online ordering to inviting more customer interaction through company Web sites. The rise of online ordering was also a discussion point, and a leader in this area is Papa John's, which was one of the first companies to incorporate the system into its business model. The company said this ordering system is gaining traction with both consumers and franchisees, which are beginning to see it succeed.

Rothenberg notes that the Internet is not only being used as an online ordering system. He says many operators are using it to remotely manage their restaurants. POS systems' information can be uploaded to a Web site and anywhere a restaurant owner can launch a browser, he or she can look at the latest restaurant metrics. "Managers can get a view in a flash of what is going on at the restaurant," Rothenberg says.

Companies are also using the Internet for another very important factor of the industry: managing customer relationships. As more consumers use the Internet to order their food online they will be given the opportunity to respond to customer surveys, receive e-mail newsletters and offers, and benefit from other marketing opportunities that tie the consumer to the restaurant, according to Rothenberg. "Consumers can sign up and companies will capture their information and link them to a transaction," he says. From there restaurants can see their consumers' demographics and who is patronizing the restaurant.

Operators will be able to see if they are reaching their target markets. It will give them an opportunity to ask the question, "Do I need to do anything differently?" The Internet allows companies to market to customers more cost efficiently, inviting them to return with offers of discounts on their favorite menu items and other ideas. "Before the Internet this type of customer tracking and marketing was a multi-million dollar campaign," Rothenberg notes. "Now it is affordable for smaller businesses."

Laws and Regulations Governing the Food Services Industry

The food services industry is a highly regulated one, and no one would want it any other way. Laws and regulations in place are designed to ensure that patrons can enter an eating establishment with confidence that the food they order and consume is safe. The United States is considered to have one of the safest food services industries in the world.

Still, food services operators have a large number of laws and regulations to adhere to. Not only do operators need to stay current on all labor and wage laws, as well as federal, state, and local tax laws, but they also need to be knowledgeable of food and health safety laws. Food must be cooked and presented at certain temperatures. Tips must be reported and restaurant owners are responsible for making sure employees are doing so. Operators are required to be certified, licensed, and insured to sell food to patrons. There are building laws, codes, and enforcements as well. Food service providers in schools and institutions are subject to even more laws and regulations. It can be an overwhelming and mind-boggling task to stay on top of all the regulations required by the industry. While the information below is a good start, it is not intended to replace your own thorough investigation of the specific laws and regulations you need to follow in your business and location.

Federal Labor and Wage Laws

Many restaurants and food service organizations hire from a younger pool of workers, ages 16 to 24, and some even hire 14- or 15-year-old kids. The employees at the lower end of that range are usually still in school and laws specify how many hours they are legally able to work and what kind of jobs they can do. According to the United States Department of Labor, 14- and 15-year-olds are only allowed to work between 7:00 A.M. and 7:00 P.M. outside of school hours. Kids this age can only work 3 hours on school days, 8 hours on non-school days, and 18 hours in school weeks, 40 hours a week on non-school weeks. Between June 1 and Labor Day kids in this age group can work until 9:00 P.M.

The laws are not so specific when it comes to the 16- to 18-year-old age group . In fact there are no federal laws governing how many hours and when kids age 16 and older can work. However, there are some restrictions about the type of jobs kids under age 18 can work. Kids who are 16- and 17-years-old may only perform non-hazardous jobs. Kids who are 14- and 15-years old may work outside school hours in various nonmanufacturing, non-mining, and nonhazardous jobs. Employers may be required to provide proof of an employee's age, so they must make sure that they have a copy of their employees' driver's license, learner's permit, state ID, or certification of age.

All employees regardless of age should be paid at least minimum wage. There are some exceptions, however, and they can be a bit tricky. For example, a special minimum wage of $4.25 per hour applies to employees under the age of 20 during their first 90 consecutive calendar days of employment with an employer. After 90 days, the Fair Labor Standards Act (FLSA) requires employers to pay the full federal minimum wage, which is $7.25 per hour worked.

Full-time students in specific circumstances also can be paid less than minimum wage. Employers that hire full-time students employed in retail or service stores, farms, or colleges and universities can obtain a certificate from the United States Department of Labor which allows the student to be paid no less than 85 percent of the minimum wage. The certificate also limits the hours that the student may work to 8 hours in a day and no more than 20 hours a week when school is in session, and 40 hours per week when school is out, and requires the employer to follow all child labor laws. Once students graduate or leave school for good, they must be paid at least the federal minimum wage.

There is another scenario that allows employers to pay less than minimum wage. Under the Student Learners Program, high school students who are at least 16 years old and who are enrolled in vocational education may be paid no less than 75 percent of the minimum wage, provided the employer obtains a certificate from the U.S. Department of Labor. Many high schools now offer vocational programs like this in the hospitality and food services industry and students work at a specific restaurant as part of their vocational training. Employers interested in applying for a student learner certificate should contact the Department of Labor Wage and Hour Regional Office with jurisdiction over their state.

What about wage laws for adults? Are there any special regulations for adults in the food services industry? An employer of a tipped employee is only required to pay $2.13 an hour in direct wages if that amount plus the tips received equals at least the federal

On the Cutting Edge

Online Ordering

Studies have shown that more than 30 percent of casual dining customers use the Web sites of their favorite restaurants to gather information or place orders. Not surprisingly, 51 percent of quick service experts agree that online ordering is "the next big thing," according to *QSR Magazine*. "What's happened is that restaurants are realizing that more people are doing online ordering and have high-speed access," says Rob Saunders, director of marketing for Dotmenu Corporation, New York, New York. "At this point restaurants almost have to have online ordering."

minimum wage. The employee retains all tips and the employee customarily and regularly receives more than $30 a month in tips. If an employee's tips combined with the employer's direct wages of at least $2.13 an hour do not equal the federal minimum hourly wage, the employer must make up the difference. There are also state regulations that employers must take into consideration as well. Some states have minimum wage laws specific to tipped employees. When an employee is subject to both federal and state wage laws, the employee is entitled to the provisions that provide the greater benefits. So operators must take state regulations into account before setting wages.

In addition to tips affecting minimum wage, employers in food services operations also have to ensure that their employees are reporting their tips on their taxes, and are withholding taxes from them. Businesses are also required to report tips on the business tax return as well. This can become burdensome for both employer and employee. Employees have been encouraged to keep daily logs of the tips they receive and report them to the employer. In 2007 the IRS responded to the food services industry's complaint that tip reporting was having a negative impact on the industry. It started the Attributed Tip Income Program (ATIP). ATIP reduces industry recordkeeping burdens, has simple enrollment requirements, and promotes reporting tips on federal income tax returns. ATIP is similar to previous programs, except in a few important ways: ATIP does not require employers to meet with the IRS to determine tip rates or eligibility, employers are not required to sign an agreement with the IRS to participate, and like other tip reporting programs, participation by employers and their employees is voluntary.

Employers who participate in ATIP report the tip income of employees based on a formula that uses a percentage of gross receipts, which are generally attributed among employees based on the practices of the restaurant. Employees are then not required to keep daily logs of their tips. While participating in ATIP employees are not subject to tax examination by the IRS. Not all operations qualify for the program. The bottom line is that all employees that receive more than $20 per month in tips must report 100 percent of those tips on their taxes or both the employee and restaurant may be subject to an audit.

Food and Health Safety Laws

Not only are restaurant owners required to know food safety, but they are also required to keep their employees safe. After all, kitchen staff members are working with equipment that could cause injuries. Slick floors and other potential hazards could cause accidents to both staff members and guests. An operator needs to have a plan in place to meet all safety and Occupational Safety and Health Administration (OSHA) requirements. Additionally operators have to pass local health codes to be able to receive certification to serve food. In addition, since September 11, 2001, the United States Food and Drug Administration has published information on how retail food outlets and food service operations can reduce the risk of food tampering and terrorist efforts.

When it comes to safe food handling, kitchen staff members must be educated on the basics. This is not only important from a regulation standpoint, but from the customer's viewpoint as well. In a recent poll conducted by Michigan State University's Food Safety Policy Center, 63 percent of Americans say they are very or fairly concerned about the safety of the food they eat.

The primary guidance for food safety in food services kitchens comes from the United States Food and Drug Administration's Center for Food Safety and Applied Nutrition. The Center publishes Hazard Analysis and Critical Control Point (HACCP), which details seven principles for preventing foodborne illness. These seven principles were originally developed more than 30 years ago for the space program to keep astronauts' food safe for consumption. HAACP is widely used throughout the industry today. The seven principles are described as follows, courtesy of the FDA's Center for Food Safety and Applied Nutrition Web site:

1. Analyze hazards. Potential hazards associated with a food and measures to control those hazards are identified. The hazard could be biological, such as a microbe; chemical, such as a toxin; or physical, such as ground glass or metal fragments.
2. Identify critical control points. These are points in a food's production, from its raw state through processing and shipping to consumption by the consumer, at which the potential hazard can be controlled or eliminated. Examples are cooking, cooling, packaging, and metal detection.
3. Establish preventive measures with critical limits for each control point. For a cooked food, for example, this might include setting the minimum cooking temperature and time required to ensure the elimination of any harmful microbes.
4. Establish procedures to monitor the critical control points. Such procedures might include determining how and by whom cooking time and temperature should be monitored.
5. Establish corrective actions to be taken when monitoring shows that a critical limit has not been met. For example, reprocessing or disposing of food if the minimum cooking temperature is not met.
6. Establish procedures to verify that the system is working properly. For example, testing time-and-temperature recording devices to verify that a cooking unit is working properly.
7. Establish effective recordkeeping to document the HACCP system. This would include records of hazards and their control methods, the monitoring of safety requirements, and action taken to correct potential problems. Each of these principles must be backed by sound scientific knowledge: for example, published microbiological studies on time and temperature factors for controlling foodborne pathogens.

Establishing an HACCP system is important in meeting food safety requirements, but operators also have to make sure they pass local health inspections. Each food service operation needs to apply for a license to serve food in its chosen location and meet all local guide-lines, which can vary from state to state and even county to county. There are also fees associated with obtaining the license that should be part of the establishment's budget. Typically operators should be prepared to present information like a detailed drawing of the area used by the business, including all entrances and exits and a state-ment indicating the seating capacity and square footage; the location and type of all plumbing fixtures, including sinks, grease traps, and the location and size of the hot water tanks; a floor plan showing the location of fixtures, and equipment; a list of all floor, wall, and ceiling finishes; a list of all food equipment with the manufacturer and model numbers listed; and a copy of the menu.

Food safety rules (in addition to HACCP) must be communicated and posted. These include hand washing rules, safe cooking temper-atures, hair restraint requirements, safe food storage and handling requirements, health requirements of the employees, cleaning and maintenance guidelines, and other information. Details are avail-able at local health departments. Each state has detailed food safety requirements for food service establishments. For example, Ohio Administrative Code provides a 125-page document on state regu-lations for food services establishments. It is up to each individual operator and his or her staff to make sure the operation is meeting all state and local regulations.

One way to learn the ins and outs of the extensive laws and regu-lations governing food safety is to take advantage of the National Restaurant Association's ServSafe program. ServSafe is a program that teaches food safety basics and it is offered nationwide through employers, state restaurant associations, or online. After successfully completing the program employees are ServSafe certified. The pro-gram focuses on four key areas: basic food safety, personal hygiene, cross-contamination and allergens, and cleaning and sanitation. It provides the training resources to help keep food safety an essential ingredient of every meal.

Laws governing employee safety are found at the United States Department of Labor's division of Occupational Safety and Health Administration. On the OSHA Web site food service employers can find the specific laws and regulations governing the food services industry. OSHA's primary goal is to ensure that all employees have a safe work environment. Potential hazards are identified and policies for minimizing their risks are detailed. OSHA also includes a lot of information specifically for teen safety, since so many teens work at food operations. The National Institute for Occupational Safety and Health (NIOSH) estimates that in 2003 alone, 54,800 work-related injuries and illnesses among youth less than 18 years of age were treated in hospital emergency departments. Because only one-third of work-related injuries are seen in emergency departments, it is likely the actual number of such injuries among working youth is much higher; some estimates are as high as 160,000 injuries and illnesses each year. The vast majority of these injuries occur in eating and drinking establishments. The restaurant industry and other retail businesses rank high among United States industries for risk of adolescent worker injuries. Operators need to pay close attention to regulations to ensure the safety of teen employees as well as other employees.

Current Legal Issues

There are several pending laws and regulations that may impact the industry, either negatively or positively. These descriptions are courtesy of the National Restaurant Association.

The Americans with Disabilities Act (ADA) Notification Act would give business operators 90 days to review and correct alleged accessibility problems. It also would protect businesses during that time from lawsuits that allege ADA violations.

The Alternative Minimum Tax is an income tax system the United States Congress created in the late 1960s to ensure that individuals and corporations earning above certain income thresholds could not use tax deductions, exclusions, and other loopholes to avoid paying a minimum amount of taxes. Thousands of small businesses and millions of middle-income Americans now face AMT liability because Congress does not regularly increase the income threshold.

Business Meal Deductibility is seen as an issue by restaurants. Business meal deductions are currently limited to 50 percent of costs. The National Restaurant Association's position is that doing business over a meal is the only means of marketing and advertising for many small businesses and self-employed individuals and that it is a legitimate deduction that should be fully deductible.

Another issue that could have a huge impact on the industry is the Employee Free Choice Act. Currently employees are entitled to a private-ballot election when deciding whether they want union representation in their workplace. Elections are overseen by the National Labor Relations Board (NLRB), which has numerous procedures in place to ensure fair, fraud-free elections. Because of NLRB safeguards, employees can cast their votes confidentially, without peer pressure or coercion from unions or employers.

If Congress passes the Employee Free Choice Act, employees effectively lose their right to private-ballot elections. The bill would establish what the Act is calling a "card-check" union organizing system, in which a majority of employees simply sign a card in favor of union representation. The measure would also require a government-mandated arbitrator to force a contract if the employer and the union do not reach an agreement within 120 days.

Several legislative acts are pending in relation to food safety. While no bills have cleared Congress as of December 2009, action is being discussed on several fronts. One being considered is expanding the FDA's capacity. Some critics argue that the FDA does not have the resources or authority it needs to do its job. John Dingell (D-Mich.) and others have suggested a range of proposals, including increasing FDA funding, holding the FDA more accountable for food-safety results, giving the agency authority to issue mandatory recalls, and empowering the FDA to create national food registries for adulterated foods and require everyone in the food chain—restaurants included—to report to that registry.

A second area being looked at is ensuring the safety of imported foods. An estimated $2 trillion in imported products entered the United States in 2008 and experts expect that amount to triple by 2015. A top-level White House interagency working group released its first report on import safety in September 2008. The report advocates that the United States move toward a risk-based, prevention-focused model rather than relying on the current system of "snapshots" at the border to interdict unsafe products. Since other countries' food safety systems are not as rigorous as the United States' there is quite a bit of risk associated with imported foods.

A third area under consideration by lawmakers is improving produce safety. Recent large, multistate foodborne-illness outbreaks linked to contaminated produce have increased public concern about the safety of fresh produce. One example is the outbreak of salmonellosis that occurred in jars of salsa in 2008, and another outbreak of salmonellosis that occurred in peanut butter in 2009. In both cases these items were recalled from grocery store shelves. Senate Agriculture Committee Chairman Tom Harkin (D-Iowa) is working on a produce safety bill that will include mandatory regulation of the fresh produce industry—which the industry itself has called for.

INTERVIEW

The Rise of Prepared Foods

Jim Grote
Founder and CEO of Donato's Pizza, based in Columbus, Ohio

In your opinion what is the current state of the food service industry and how did it get there?
Since I began in the early sixties the scheduled family meals have given way to the convenience of ready-to-eat food due to the influence of both parents working along with after school activities, especially sports for the kids. Each family member seems to be on a variety of schedules and meals are revolving around these schedules.

These and other cultural changes have contributed to the tremendous rise in the demand for prepared food consumed away from home and at home. All meal occasions have benefited from this demand, including breakfast, lunch, dinner, and late night. With the increased demand for prepared foods comes the desire for meal variety, resulting in many new concepts.

I believe that food service is continually growing, but individual segments will expand or contract with economic conditions. As disposable income shrinks, the consumer is still demanding price, quality, and service. Because they have less income, they are very discerning about where they spend their dollars. As an example, a customer would say that a product isn't the very best quality, but for the money it is good enough. In good times, a customer may say, "I want the best quality and I am willing to pay for it."

What are some of the newest trends in the industry that will really gain momentum over the next few years?
[There will be] continued development of wholesome, healthy food that tastes good. More and more consumers will demand transparency about the ingredients in their food and the quality and healthfulness of those ingredients.

At Donato's, we've introduced a variety of more healthful menu items in the past few years, we've removed trans fat from our products before it was mandated, and we'll continue to develop products that not only taste good, but are good for you as well.

As labor costs increase, more food will be prepared in a central location and distributed to restaurants for customization of individual orders.

Labeling is also an issue for the industry. Labeling menu items is something some operators want and others do not. The National Restaurant Association supports labeling, and is urging members of Congress to co-sponsor the Labeling Education and Nutrition Act of 2008 (LEAN Act), which will provide a national nutrition labeling standard for food service establishments with 20 or more locations. National Restaurant Association research has shown that Americans are seeking to eat more healthfully when they dine out. While many restaurant chains have responded to this trend by offering nutrition information, state and local policymakers have reacted by passing menu-labeling laws. Instead, the LEAN Act proposes that the federal government should set a single national standard for nutrition-information disclosure for chain food service companies. Such a uniform national nutrition standard will allow consumers access to detailed nutrition information that meets their needs while providing clarity, consistency, and flexibility for restaurants in how that information is provided.

This list of pending issues is nowhere near exhaustive. One thing is clear: The industry is complex and so are the laws and regulations governing it. Being a member of an industry association or reading trade publications providing regular updates and information is critical for understanding the issues that may affect an operation's bottom line and day-to-day business. These associations also feature conferences, seminars, and other educational and networking opportunities that keep people in the field apprised of the latest trends and technologies, a key factor of career success.

Key Conferences and Industry Events

Many people may think industry events are a waste of time, but they should think again. Conferences, seminars, and events can benefit employees in many ways. First, every industry is constantly changing, and the food services industry is no exception. It can take a lot of work to keep up with all the trends and changes occurring on a nearly daily basis. Attending important conferences and events keeps you informed of all the latest developments in the industry.

Also, never underestimate the value of networking. In today's tough economy it is more important than ever before to maintain relationships with others in the industry. "Networking is certainly important," says Karen Ickes, senior vice president of human resources for Wendy's International. Ickes says that in the current job market, when a company advertises for a position it is flooded with applications. One of the best ways to stand out from the crowd is networking—knowing someone at the company who can recommend you. Attending industry conferences and events is one of the best ways to meet others in the industry and expand your network.

Key industry conferences are also informative about career development and marketing yourself within the industry. Often events offer continuing education and certification courses, one-on-one mentoring and meetings with key leaders in the industry, and opportunities to talk to others about how they are successfully dealing with issues in the industry. All in all, choosing to attend the right industry events can lead to more opportunities down the road. Here are some of the conferences and events to consider.

All Things Organic Conference and Trade Show   Given the growing popularity and demand for organic products, this is an important event for food services professionals. In three days, participants can meet with more than 300 organic suppliers offering the right products to grow their businesses. Attendees can network with thousands of business professionals, exhibitors, and organic companies to obtain ideas that are critical to the success of their businesses. (http://www.organicexpo.com)

American Culinary Federation Annual Conference   The American Culinary Federation describes its annual conference as the biggest annual gathering of chefs, students, and food service professionals in the United States. An array of workshops, seminars, cooking demonstrations, networking opportunities, and social functions are part of this convention that takes place in July. (http://www.acfchefs.org)

American Hotel & Lodging Association Summer Summit   This association for operators in the hotel and lodging segment of the industry offers members committee meetings, educational programming, networking opportunities, and the AH&LA Stars of the Industry Awards luncheon. The association says this is a prime opportunity to get involved in a committee while getting to know industry leaders in an intimate setting. This yearly event takes place in June. (http://www.ahla.com)

American Society for Healthcare Food Service Administrators National Convention   ASHFSA is affiliated with one of the largest organizations in heath care today, the American

Hospital Association. ASHFSA says that it is the premier source of professional education and networking for food and nutrition service management professionals. The ASHFSA conference, which usually takes place in May, blends a celebration of the past with a look into the future. The conference highlights four basic cornerstones of the industry: market, menu, management/personnel, and material/equipment. (http://www.ashfsa.org)

Association of Correctional Food Service Affiliates International Conference   The ACFSA 2009 International Conference offers attendees the opportunity to stay on top of the latest developments in correctional food service through presentations, informative roundtables, a vendor show, networking opportunities, and more. ACFSA says correctional food service is a fast-moving profession and attending the 2009 International Conference, which takes place in August, is an excellent way to learn and advance professional and personal growth.   (http://www.acfsa.org/events.php)

Commercial Food Equipment Service Association Fall Conference   CFESA holds biannual conferences in the spring and fall of each year. The Fall Conference takes place in conjunction with the NAFEM Show and will vary by location. The benefits of attending the CFESA conference include networking within the food service industry, guest speakers, high quality presentations, interactive workshops, stimulating discussion and feedback, workshops and seminars, and roundtable and group meetings. (http://www.cfesa.com)

Council of Hotel and Restaurant Trainers Semi-Annual Conference   This conference calls itself the premier gathering of hotel trainers, restaurant trainers, and human resource professionals. Professionals meet to learn from inspiring keynote speakers, participate in interactive educational breakout sessions, network together, and share best practices. The three-day conference is packed with informative sessions designed to help hotel and restaurant training professionals solve key issues facing the hospitality industry. This event takes place in July. (http://www.chart.org/?x=events_upcoming_conferences)

Dine America Executive Idea Exchange   Dine America is the conference that brings restaurant executives together to exchange ideas designed to bring customers to their stores. Dine America invites a select group of industry executives, so participants can be sure they will interact with some of the best minds in the business.

This event takes place in September and explores how operators can build their businesses not only with but in spite of the market. (http://www.dineamerica.us)

Food Marketing Institute's Future Connect   Usually occurring each May, the Food Marketing Institute offers attendees three educational tracks: operations, executive, and senior executive. The highly interactive and collaborative format mixes strategically focused general sessions with hands-on, university-style case studies and work groups. The program includes content that focuses on three primary business areas: performance, people, and profit. Performance Connect is a program designed to improve the participant's contribution to the company. Focus is on individual growth, personal development, and professional effectiveness. People Connect hones people management skills. The focus is on how to motivate and improve the performance of all employees, including direct and indirect reports, colleagues, and teammates. Profit Connect optimizes the performance of the participant's team, department, store, division, and company. Focus is on understanding the financial picture and how people across the company can make an impact. (http://www.fmi.org)

Food Safety Summit   The Food Safety Summit, which typically occurs each April, is the largest and most established food safety and defense exposition in North America. The Summit features a full program of intensive educational seminars, workshops, networking events, and a large trade show exhibition. (http://www.foodsafetysummit.com)

Foodservice Consultants Society International Worldwide Conference   This organization that supports food service consultants offers its worldwide conference each year in China, usually in October. Participants are offered educational and networking opportunities unique to those in a consulting capacity. The conference was also one of the first to "go green" and achieved a certificate for its carbonless footprint. (http://www.fcsi.org)

Healthcare Foodservice Management Annual Conference Each August HFM presents dynamic, award-winning international speakers, informational lunch sessions, educational breakout sessions, a silent auction theme party, and exciting HFM culinary competitions. HFM says this is attendees' opportunity to meet other health care food service leaders from across North America; network with peers; and learn about new trends, critical issues, and challenges facing operators today. (http://www.hfm.org)

Institute of Food Technologists Annual Meeting and Food Expo   The IFT says this annual June meeting is the largest annual food science forum and exposition in the world. More than 20,000 food scientists, suppliers, marketers, and others from around the globe meet at the convention, attracted by the promise of encountering the driving forces behind the innovations and information affecting consumers, growers, processors, regulators, and researchers who make the U.S. food supply diverse. Experts from companies, government agencies, and research institutions provide insight during more than 1,000 presentations covering topics ranging from new health and safety benefits and product innovations to the latest consumer favorites, fears, and trends. Approximately 1,000 companies regularly present their latest advancements for making food more fun, functional, nutritious, appealing, or accessible. (http://www.ift.org)

Institute for Supply Management Hospitality Supply Management Conference   ISM's mission is to lead the supply management profession to achieve excellence through research, promotional activities, and education. The ISM believes that in today's challenging environment, it is critical for supply managers to bring more value to their organizations. The Hospitality Supply Management Conference helps supply professionals gain new perspectives while networking with colleagues and industry leaders. Professionals can discover upcoming trends, discuss best practices, and learn about current trends and innovations in sustainability, disaster planning, and food safety. The event typically occurs in May. (http://www.ism.ws/education/content.cfm?ItemNumber=18844)

International Association of Culinary Professionals Annual International Conference   IACP members from around the globe gather each April for several days of networking, learning, and information exchange at this conference. Attendees include longtime and brand new IACP members. IACP promises that there are always new connections to make, myriad opportunities to hone skills, and, of course, unparalleled food experiences to enjoy. New trends in the industry are addressed, as well as their impacts on members. (http://www.iacp.com)

International Foodservice Distributors Association Distribution Solutions Conference   This event is important for those in the distribution side of the industry. The primary goal of the conference is to provide educational opportunities to executives and professionals in the industry. Attendees can hear from peers about technologies and business practices that can improve long-term competitiveness, access a unique exposition featuring the latest products and services supporting distributor operations, plus take advantage of facility tours and networking events. The conference includes a balance of sessions that meet the diverse needs of food service distributors, and provides timely topics for broadliners as well as system and specialty distributors. Educational topics include the newest methods for improving efficiencies, and implementing and leveraging existing practices and technologies. This annual conference typically occurs in October. (http://www.ifdaonline.org)

International Food Service Executives Association Annual International Conference and Seminar This conference for industry executives takes place each March. This association and conference is all about developing leaders and their leadership skills and abilities. Training and classes for certification and networking are a large part of the conference. Executives are encouraged to receive certification as master executives in the industry. (http://www.ifsea.com)

International Foodservice Manufacturers Association Foodservice Fundamentals Seminar IFMA offers the Foodservice Fundamental Series of educational programs for individuals who are new to or have just recently entered the food service industry. This series offers three separate programs ranging from an introduction and overview of the food service marketplace through advanced comprehensive courses for more experienced members, which are focused on the various supply-chain members. Seminars occur throughout the year. (http://www.ifmaworld.com)

International Foodservice Manufacturers Association Presidents Conference Each November executives involved in food service manufacturing gather to interact with other food service leaders. The IFMA says that this conference offers an unsurpassed opportunity to connect with operator and distributor customers and gain insights that executives can incorporate into strategic planning. Past discussions and activities included an analysis of current political and cultural headlines and their impact on the country's future, perspectives from leading food service and business authorities, peer-to-peer interaction with operator and distributor supply-chain partners, and networking events designed

to widen participants' circle of business contacts. (http://www
.ifmaworld.com)

International Foodservice Technology Expo and Conference
Technology is changing the way operators do business in nearly
every facet of the industry. This conference, which occurs in February, presents the effective use of technology and how it can
deliver powerful gains in productivity and profits for food service
companies. The event connects technology decision-makers to
profit-making I.T. solutions. It offers ideas for using food service
technology to help organizations spark sales, increase efficiency,
and pump up profits. (http://www.fstec.com)

**International Hotel & Restaurant Association Annual Con-
gress**   Each October members of this international organization
meet to discuss global issues affecting the industry. The three-day
event provides education and networking for worldwide hospitality executives. The 2008 congress covered sustainable development and climate change and hospitality. (http://www.ih-ra
.com)

**National Association of College and University Food Services
Conference**   The National Association of College and University
Food Services assists members and advances the collegiate food
service industry by providing insight, education, services, and
knowledge exchange. At the conference the NACUFS says learning will be fun and easy. The conference, which takes place in
July, offers a wide variety of speakers and sessions as well as the
conference's Culinary Challenge. (http://www.nacufs.org)

**National Restaurant Association Restaurant, Hotel-Motel
Show**   This event is considered the largest industry trade event
in the world. It takes place each May and offers attendees access
to the newest innovations in equipment and technology, sixty-
five free educational seminars, and free personalized consulting.
Celebrity chefs like Ming Tsai share their insights with attendees.
(htpp://show.restaurant.org)

Natural Products Association Natural MarketPlace   Considering the growing popularity and demand for organic and natural
products, this is an important event for food services professionals. The MarketPlace features a trade show floor with more than
400 exhibits of the latest natural products and services alongside
special events, activities, and a highly rated education program
featuring leading experts. The Natural Products Association says

Natural MarketPlace is a powerful selling, networking, and educational opportunity, allowing attendees to source new products, build industry relationships, and connect with more than 4,500 colleagues. (http://www.naturalmarketplaceshow.com)

North American Association of Food Equipment Manufacturers Trade Show   NAFEM's biennial trade show attracts approximately 20,000 food service professionals and features more than 600 North American manufacturers. In addition to educational and networking opportunities, participants are able to get a preview of some of the latest innovations in food service equipment in the trade show's gallery. The gallery showcases products that address areas of greatest operator concern, including labor and cost savings, energy efficiency, food safety, and sanitation. The trade show usually takes place in February. (http://www.nafem.org/thenafemshow)

Prepared Foods New Product Conference   With more operators in all segments of the industry turning to prepared foods as a source of menu options, this conference can keep you up to date on the latest products. The Prepared Foods Network offers suppliers an integrated and innovative portfolio of magazines, annual directories, conferences, newsletters, and Internet-based products designed to ensure the successful marketing of their products. Prepared Foods Network calls this conference the food and beverage industry's premier event, where R&D, marketing, and executive management professionals gather to gain valuable insights into new food and beverage products and exciting new consumer trends around the world. (http://www.bnpevents.com)

Produce Marketing Association Foodservice Conference and Exposition   The PMA's three-day learning and networking conference, which takes place in July, is focused on bringing food service professionals together to learn about produce industry issues and topics, see the latest products and services, and strengthen relationships. Attendees meet face-to-face with food service leaders from throughout the supply chain, including chefs, restaurant owners and operators, food service distributors, wholesalers, consultants, packers, and industry product and service providers. (http://www.pma.com/foodservice/2010l)

School Nutrition Association Annual National Conference   According to SNA this is the largest and most important annual gathering for the K–12 school nutrition profession. It offers more than 80 quality education sessions, which SNA guarantees will provide attendees with new perspectives and practices. Also, the conference's exhibit hall contains information and ideas, new products to boost participation, equipment to help streamline production, and materials to expand a program's summer service. SNA also says the conference is participants' best opportunity to meet face to face with thousands of operators from districts across the nation. (http://docs.schoolnutrition.org/meetingsandevents)

Summer Fancy Food Show   This is one of North America's largest specialty food shows. It takes place in June and presents new ideas and new products to keep menus fresh and innovative. Highlights include 140,000 specialty foods and beverages, 2,300 exhibitors from 75 countries, and more than 20 customized educational seminars, tastings, cooking classes, and tours. (http://www.specialtyfood.com)

Women Chefs and Restaurateurs Annual Conference   Each November this event for women in the industry provides networking opportunities, high-level educational sessions, and exciting keynote presentations. The goal of the organization is to support women in the industry. (http://www.womenchefs.org)

World Pastry Forum   The World Pastry Forum is a series of classes and seminars taught by international leaders of the pastry industry. At the forum top chefs from around the globe converge to teach new and exciting classes. Attendees can learn innovative techniques that will be used throughout the industry and network with the best pastry chefs and industry suppliers. The World Pastry Forum offers participants the full experience to excel as a pastry chef. Attendees can choose demonstrations and intensive hands-on programs. (http://forums.worldpastryforum.com/events)

Chapter 3

On the Job

Most people are attracted to the food services industry for two reasons: a love of food, and an enjoyment of working with people. Whether you are an accountant, information technology professional, or creative chef, there is a place for you in the industry. As a worker in one of the nation's largest industries you can take your pick of location, restaurant, or branch of the industry. If restaurants or noncommercial food service is not your first choice of career, there are industry suppliers, equipment manufacturers, food safety specialists, nutritionists, attorneys, and engineering jobs. The industry is always in need of creative, energetic people with fresh ideas and dedication.

Below you will find an A-through-Z listing, broken up by industry segment, of the jobs available in the industry today. Each listing will describe the job, its level (entry, mid-, etc.), education or certification needed, if there are any direct reports associated with the job, and the career path associated with it. That way you can easily chart your path to your end career destination.

Administrative and Professional

Accountant

Accounting is an important function for any operation, large or small. Often accounts tie in to inventory, human resource management, and other measurements of operational efficiency.

Small restaurant owners may hire accounting firms to manage this function or do the basics themselves. Large food service corporations, multi-unit operations, and larger independent restaurants may employ in-house accountants or Certified Public Accountants (CPAs) to ensure accounting is accurate, meets federal, state, and local regulations, and is providing the reporting necessary for management to make ongoing decisions. There may be positions available at all levels, entry, mid-, and executive. Most accounting positions require a college education. Some may require a CPA. Experience as an accountant or CPA in the food service industry is usually required or considered a plus. If the company has a team of accountants and accounting clerks, there may be some employees reporting to the accountant. Supervisory and management positions may be available. In large operations this career path could lead to executive positions, such as chief financial officer.

Fast
Facts

Salaries in the Food Services Industry

Here are some average salaries for chefs and cooks as of May 2006, according to the United States Bureau of Labor Statistics:

Among chefs and head cooks:
- Median annual wage-and-salary earnings were $34,370.
- The highest 10 percent earned more than $60,730.
- The middle 50 percent earned between $25,910 and $46,040.
- The lowest 10 percent earned less than $20,160.

Among fast-food cooks:
- Median annual wage-and-salary earnings were $15,410.
- The highest 10 percent earned more than $20,770.
- The middle 50 percent earned between $13,730 and $17,700.
- The lowest 10 percent earned less than $12,170.

Communications/Public Relations

This area of employment is typically found at the corporate level. A communications and/or public relations employee will be responsible for writing or editing communications for both internal and external audiences, such as company newsletters and news releases. This department may be responsible for interacting with the media or reviewing marketing and advertising material. There may be positions available at all levels, entry, mid-, and executive, depending on the size of the organization. A college degree in a related field, such as communications or journalism is required. Certifications or accreditation are not required to obtain employment, but are available through the Public Relations Society of America (http://www.prsa.org). Public relations professionals must have excellent communication skills, including writing and public speaking skills. Some companies require previous experience, depending on the level of the position. Some positions may require event planning or project management skills or background. Supervisory and management positions may be responsible for supervising other staff members in the department. In large companies communications department team members may be promoted to supervisory or management positions. Executive positions may also be available. Marketing and advertising may also fall under the jurisdiction of the communications department.

Consultant

Consultants in the industry may be self-employed or part of a consulting firm. They are hired by restaurants and institutions that may want to improve a particular facet of business, such as customer service or customer traffic. This would be either a mid- or executive level position. A college degree along with several years of experience is usually required for consultants. Other consultants may be retired restaurant entrepreneurs or operators with no formal education, but a long track record of success. Certifications are not required to obtain employment or clients, but consultants are expected to stay current on trends in the industry that could impact their clients. The Food Service Consultants Society International offers ongoing education and standards for its members. Consultants should have extensive knowledge and experience in the industry along with excellent communication and organizational skills. Consultants may have staff members working for them. If the consultant is self-employed there are no promotional opportunities, of course, but if hired by a consulting firm, there may be management and executive positions available.

Engineering/Design/Construction

Many restaurant chains, food manufacturers, and other segments of the industry are frequently building, remodeling, or redesigning their facilities. Food service operations come with their own unique requirements and challenges and engineers, designers, and construction specialists work to meet all company and government requirements and regulations. Opportunities for employees in this field are also available at construction and design firms that specialize in construction for the food service industry. These are considered mid-level positions and higher. College degrees in related fields are usually required. Engineers, designers, and construction managers will be required to have some on-the-job experience. Professional certifications or accreditations depend on the job. Companies will also want employees to have some interest in or experience with the food service industry. Engineers, designers, and construction personnel may be responsible for supervising other staff members. Employees can advance to management and executive positions, depending on the size and need of the company.

Facilities/Maintenance

Responsibilities for this field in the food service industry depend on the employer. A single-location, independent restaurant may hire a facilities person to do everything from clean the building to maintain and repair equipment. At larger food service corporations facilities employees may be responsible for maintaining several locations, as well as making sure they meet all building and safety codes. There may be positions available at every level, depending on the size of the company or restaurant. Education required for most positions is a high school diploma, vocational education, plus on-the-job experience. Supervisors and managers, especially those in charge of many facilities and employees, may be required to have a college degree plus supervisory experience. Employees will be expected to have good communication skills, a driver's license, and mechanical skills. Employees in most positions will not have direct reports, unless they are working in a supervisory capacity. In some larger operations supervisory and management positions may be available.

Executive Management

Executive level personnel are expected to lead an organization and ensure it meets measurable objectives. They are considered the visionaries that can take a company to new levels of success. They must also be able to communicate effectively and inspire others in the organization to excel. This is an executive level position. Executives are expected to have advanced degrees in business or hospitality management as well as several years of demonstrated success as a leader in the industry. An executive will have several direct reports. Executives are usually at the top of their chosen fields, but may be promoted to even higher executive levels or top positions within their companies if they are successful.

Human Resources Representative

Human resources professionals are responsible for recruiting and hiring high-quality employees. They are also often responsible for knowing federal and state employment regulations and ensuring that they are being met throughout the organization. Human resources personnel may also conduct salary reviews and assist departments and the company with maintaining a competitive edge when it comes to hiring employees. There are positions at all levels available in this facet of the industry. A college degree in human resource management, business, or related field is required. Most employers prefer employees with previous human resources experience. Higher level positions will also require supervisory or management experience. Human resources professionals are expected to possess excellent communication and people skills. Certifications are not required to obtain employment, but may be preferred. They are available through the Society for Human Resource Management (http://www.shrm.org). Entry-level positions usually do not have direct reports, but higher level positions may be responsible for supervising other staff members. In large operations there is plenty of room for growth for the human resources professional. Departments typically have several layers of management from supervisor to manager, director, and vice president, allowing many promotional opportunities.

Information Technology Professional

Information technology (IT) professionals can find many opportunities in the food service industry. Smaller independent operations often outsource this function, but larger operations and chains need in-house technology gurus as technology figures prominently as a means of order and service delivery. IT professionals may write computer programs to meet company needs, maintain computers and networks, phone equipment, and POS equipment. There are positions available at all levels. A college degree plus appropriate software and network certifications may be required depending on the specific job. Employers also prefer professionals with some on-the-job experience. In addition to technical skills, IT professionals may need to possess excellent communication, organizational, and project management skills. Supervisors and managers will have direct reports. IT departments offer promotions in the form of managerial positions. Also, as technical skills increase and professionals earn additional certifications, employees may earn promotions.

Interior Designer

Designers are responsible for creating the interiors for current and future restaurant concepts. They must be able to create a design that meets the requirements for the specific goals of the restaurant. For example, fast-food designs will be much different than fine-dining establishments. In the restaurant industry designers can find jobs at larger corporations as well as design firms. These positions are considered mid- to executive level. Employees are required to have a postsecondary education in design through a college or design school. Certifications are not required to obtain employment, but are available through the American Society of Interior Designers (http://www.interiors.org). Designers will be expected to be creative, knowledgeable, and possess excellent communication and organizational skills. A designer usually does not have direct reports but may be expected to supervise installations of fixtures and equipment. In large corporations and design firms managerial positions may be available, from supervisory roles through executive levels.

Inventory/Supplies Coordinator or Manager

This is a position most often found in chain operations, where buyers are necessary to purchase food and restaurant supplies. People working in these jobs are expected to keep inventory at levels at which no critical item runs out, yet are not overstocked so that inventory spoils or is not utilized. Purchasing professionals must consider price, quality, availability, reliability, and technical support when choosing suppliers and merchandise. To be effective, purchasing specialists must have a working technical knowledge of the goods or services to be purchased. There may be positions available at all levels: entry, mid-level, and executive. According to the United States Department of Labor Bureau of Labor Statistics *Occupational Outlook Handbook* (OOH), the amount of education required for these positions varies according to the size of the company. Some larger firms may require a minimum of a bachelor's degree, while upper management positions may require an MBA. According to the OOH, certifications are not required in some organizations, but are becoming increasingly important in others. Inventory and supply professionals can obtain designations of Certified Purchasing Manager, Certified Professional in Supply Management, and Accredited Purchasing Practitioner through the Institute for Supply Management (http://www.ism.ws). OOH says purchasing managers, buyers, and purchasing agents must know how to use word processing and spreadsheet software and the Internet. They must also have the ability to analyze technical data in suppliers' proposals; possess good communication, negotiation, and mathematical skills; and have the knowledge of supply-chain management and ability to perform financial analyses. Entry-level purchasing professionals will not have direct reports, but supervisors and managers may be responsible for other staff members. Depending on the size of the company and purchasing department, management and executive opportunities may exist.

Legal Representation

Large food service corporations and chain restaurants may have their own legal staff. These lawyers will be expected to keep executives apprised of all legal issues that may arise in the course of day-to-day operations. Lawyers will be expected to review all business documents and contracts, Web site and advertising material and licenses, and franchise agreements to make sure the business is protected. Legal representatives are considered mid-level to executive positions. A bachelor's degree and law degree are required. Lawyers must pass the state bar examination to be licensed to practice law in that state. Most states also require applicants to pass a separate written ethics examination. Continuing education is required. Company lawyers may have direct reports, usually administrative assistants. Executives or managers of the department will also be responsible for managing the legal team. Depending on the size of the company and purchasing department, management and executive opportunities may exist.

Marketing Representative/Supervisor/Director

Marketing department personnel are responsible for successfully marketing a restaurant or a particular product of the restaurant, depending on the size of the organization. Marketing campaigns must meet budget requirements. Personnel will develop marketing material and choose appropriate advertising and promotional outlets. Depending on the size of the organization, there may be positions available at all levels. A college degree in business with an emphasis on marketing is required. Higher level positions may require an MBA degree. Certifications are not required to obtain employment, but are available through the American Marketing Association (http://www.marketingpower.com). Lower level positions may require some previous industry experience—typically at least one to two years. Higher level positions may require advertising agency experience or extensive knowledge of marketing strategies, techniques, and channels. Mid- to higher level positions may be responsible for managing or supervising other staff members. A career path for the marketing professional is marketing coordinator or representative, promoted to marketing supervisor. A supervisor can be promoted to marketing director, and depending on the size of the organization, executive level positions may be the final step in a marketing career.

Product Research and Development

Product research and development (R&D) takes place at large chain restaurants as well as food service suppliers. In the food services industry these professionals are chefs, dieticians, or kitchen technicians that develop and test new products to roll out to company restaurants or food service customers. R&D employees are expected to produce good-tasting foods that may also be highly nutritious, and easily produced and packaged. There are positions available at all levels. According to the OOH, most research technicians need an associate's degree or a certificate in applied science or science-related technology. Technicians with a high school diploma and no college degree typically begin work as trainees under the direct supervision of a more experienced technician, and eventually earn a two year degree in science technology. No certifications are required or available for these professionals. The OOH says research and development professionals should have good communication skills because technicians are often required to report their findings both orally and in writing. Additionally technicians should be able to work well with others. Because computers often are used in research and development laboratories, technicians should also have strong computer skills, especially in computer modeling. Organizational ability, an eye for detail, and skill in interpreting scientific results are important as well, as are a high mechanical aptitude, attention to detail, and analytical thinking. Entry-level technicians will not have direct reports. However, supervisors and managers will be responsible for directing other staff members. Advancement occurs as technicians are promoted to supervisory and management roles. Depending on the size of the company, executive positions may also be available.

Quality Assurance

These positions are most often available at very large chain restaurants and food service suppliers and processors. Quality assurance workers monitor or audit products to make sure they meet company quality standards. When defects are found, quality assurance inspectors notify supervisors and help to analyze and correct the problems. Quality control positions are usually considered entry-level, but are usually only obtained after the employee has spent time in production and understands the production process. A college degree is not required, but more quality control programs require employees to have more advanced computer and technical skills, so vocational training programs are becoming available. According to OOH, training has become more formalized with the advent of standards from the International Organization for Standardization. As a result, certification as a quality inspector, offered by the American Society for Quality (http://www.asq.org), is designed to certify that someone is trained in the field and may enable workers to advance in this field. Other qualities quality assurance employees should possess include math and communication skills and good hand-eye coordination and vision. Another important skill is the ability to analyze and inter-pret data, manuals, and other material to determine specifications, inspection procedures, formulas, and methods for making adjust-ments. Entry-level positions will not have direct reports. Depend-ing on the size of the company and quality assurance department, management and executive opportunities may exist.

Real Estate and Development

Employees in this position have expertise in finding suitable real estate for future restaurant locations. They also manage exist-ing properties by renegotiating leases and assuring that the real estate meets corporate goals. Jobs in this department are consid-ered mid- to executive level positions. A college degree in busi-ness administration or management is required. Some companies require or prefer employees in these positions to have an MBA or JD, especially at executive levels. Certifications are not required to obtain employment. Real estate and development professionals are expected to have some experience in the field of corporate real estate. They are also expected to have knowledge of zoning regula-tions and standard lease terms and conditions, as well as knowl-edge of developing traditional and nontraditional sites. Managerial and financial analysis skills may also be required. Employees in these positions may have supervisory responsibilities for other staff members. Career paths at large multi-unit companies include pro-motions to supervisor, then manager. Executive level positions at large corporations include vice president and chief development officer.

Restaurant Assistant Manager

Assistant managers assist the general manager of a restaurant and ensure quality customer service, appropriate staffing levels, compli-ance with government and safety requirements, and some supervi-sion of staff. This is a mid-level position. Education requirements differ from restaurant to restaurant, though most prefer candidates with a college degree or some college education. Certifications are not required to obtain employment. Some restaurants or companies may require six months to a year of restaurant supervision expe-rience, or supervision experience in another industry. Assistant managers are expected to have excellent communication skills and the ability to interact positively with customers and employees. The assistant manager may have serving and/or kitchen staff employees reporting to him or her. The typical career path for assistant managers is a promotion to general manager at the same store or different location. If the company is a large chain operation, additional opportunities for promotion may be from general manager to district manager, and then to executive level management positions.

Restaurant Manager

The responsibilities of restaurant managers can vary from one company to another. In general the manager is responsible for all facets of the operation, from overseeing the ordering of supplies, to the preparation of the food, and overall customer experience. Managers must ensure that kitchen equipment is in working order and food and employee safety procedures are being followed. Depending on the size of the company and their policies, the managers may also be responsible for recruiting and hiring employees. Other administrative and culinary tasks such as approving employee time sheets and menu development and promotion may also be part of the manager's responsibilities. This is considered a mid-level position. According to the OOH, postsecondary education is preferred for many food service manager positions, but it is not a requirement for many others. The OOH reports that more than 40 percent of food service managers have a high school diploma or less education, and less than 25 percent have a bachelor's or graduate degree. However, a postsecondary degree is preferred by higher end full-service restaurants and for many corporate positions, such as managing a regional or national restaurant chain, or overseeing contract food service operations at sports and entertainment complexes, school campuses, and institutional facilities. Certifications are not required to obtain employment or for advancement but are available through the National Restaurant Association (http://www.restaurant.org). Managers can earn the certification of Foodservice Management Professional. This designation is most helpful to those who do not have formal education or extensive experience in the industry. Managers also need to be reliable and demonstrate they have leadership skills and can take initiative. Excellent communication and problem-solving skills are also a must for managers. Managers will have several direct reports, as well as take ultimate responsibility for the employees at the location they manage. A willingness to relocate is often essential for

Professional Ethics

How to Resign from a New Job

So you take a job you think you are going to love only to find out it is totally different than you thought it would be. You decide to bow out early. How do you tactfully resign? Human resource experts agree that in every situation honesty is the best policy. Let your boss know as soon as possible the job is not what you had expected. Do not lay blame on the company. You do not want to burn any bridges. The sooner you resign, the more likely the company can hire a replacement that was already interviewed, preventing them from having to start over with the recruiting and hiring process.

managers to advance to positions with greater responsibility, says the OOH. Managers typically advance to larger or more prominent establishments or regional management positions within restaurant chains. Some may open their own food service establishments or franchise operation.

Risk/Safety/Security Coordinators or Managers

Risk managers and those specializing in safety and security help prevent harm to workers, property, the environment, and the general public. In large food services operations and companies these specialists assess the risks associated with day-to-day operations and prepare procedures to minimize those risks. These are considered mid-level positions. The OOH says that some employers require workers specializing in this field to have a bachelor's degree in occupational health, safety, or a related field. There also are associate's degree and one-year certificate programs, which primarily are intended for technicians. According to the OOH, although voluntary, many employers encourage their employees to earn certification. Certification is available through several organizations. The Board of Certified Safety Professionals offers the Certified Safety Professional (CSP) credential. Also, the Council on Certification of Health, Environmental, and Safety Technologists certifies people as Occupational Health and

Safety Technologists (OHST), who may be called Certified Loss Control Specialists (CLCS), Construction Health and Safety Technicians (CHST), and Safety Trained Supervisors (STS) (see http://www.bcsp.org for more details). Employees in this field should be responsible and very detail-oriented. Good communication skills are also important. Entry-level positions will not have direct reports. Supervisory or management positions will. Depending on the size of the company and risk management and safety department, management and executive opportunities may exist.

Sales

Sales positions in the food services industry are primarily available at industry suppliers versus restaurants, although some food service operations have diversified and are offering packaged products to consumers at grocery stores and require sales professionals to sell these products to grocery stores. Sales representatives demonstrate their products and explain how using those products can reduce costs and increase sales. According to the OOH sales representatives stay abreast of new products and the changing needs of their customers in a variety of ways. They attend trade shows where new products and technologies are showcased. They also attend conferences and conventions to meet other sales representatives and clients and discuss new product developments. In addition, the entire sales force may participate in company-sponsored meetings to review sales performance, product development, sales goals, and profitability. There are usually positions available at all three levels. There does not appear to be any industry standard as far as education requirements. At the minimum a high school diploma and some industry experience will be required. Some companies will prefer candidates with a bachelor's degree. According to the OOH nearly 40 percent of all sales representatives (excluding retail sales people) have a college degree. Certifications are not required to obtain employment, but those employed in a food processing or manufacturing environment may want to earn a Certified Professional Manufacturers' Representative (CPMR) or the Certified Sales Professional (CSP) designation, offered by the Manufacturers' Representatives Education Research Foundation (http://www.mrerf.org). Sales representatives should be goal-oriented, be able to operate independently, and possess good organizational and communication skills. Persuasiveness and persistence are also necessary. Entry-level sales positions will not have direct reports. However, supervisors and managers will be responsible for other staff members. According to the OOH, promotions frequently take the form of an assignment to a larger account or territory where commissions are likely to be greater. Those who have good sales records and leadership ability may advance to higher level positions such as sales supervisor, district manager, or vice president of sales. Others find opportunities in purchasing, advertising, or marketing research.

Tax Specialist

Tax specialists are usually accountants that specialize in tax laws and accounting. They are primarily employed by large corporations and organizations with ongoing tax accounting needs. Tax specialists will ensure that all financial aspects of the company are properly reported on the business tax returns. They have extensive knowledge of tax laws so they can ensure that the company is taking full advantage of all deductions. This is considered a mid-level position. Most accountant and auditor positions require at least a bachelor's degree in accounting or a related field. If a tax specialist is required to file a report with the Securities and Exchange Commission (SEC), he or she is required by law to be a Certified Public Accountant (CPA). CPAs are licensed by their State Board of Accountancy. According to OOH, the Accreditation Council for Accountancy and Taxation, a satellite organization of the National Society of Accountants, confers three designations to accountants who specialize in tax accounting: Accredited Business Accountant (ABA), Accredited Tax Advisor (ATA), and Accredited Tax Preparer (ATP). Candidates for the ABA must pass an exam. Candidates for the other designations must complete the required course work and in some cases also pass an exam. Tax specialists also need to have excellent math and analytical skills. Communication skills are also important. Tax specialists will not usually have direct reports. Depending on the size of the company and the accounting department, supervisory, management, and executive level positions may be available.

Restaurant: Kitchen Staff

Baker

Bakers may be employed at restaurants, bakeries, or food suppliers or manufacturers. Bakers will need to consistently produce quality bread and baked goods for consumers or other customers. In some cases bakers may be asked to create new baked goods for restaurant or customer consumption. This is an entry-level position. The OOH says that bakers often start as apprentices or trainees. Apprentice bakers usually start in craft bakeries, while trainees usually begin in store bakeries, like those in supermarkets. Many apprentice bakers participate in correspondence study and may work toward a certificate in baking. Working as a baker's assistant or at other activities that involve handling food is also a useful way to train. The skills needed to be a baker may often be underestimated. Bakers need to know about ingredients and nutrition, government health and sanitation regulations, business concepts, applied chemistry—including how ingredients combine and how they are affected by heat and production processes—and how to operate and maintain machinery. Certifications may be required to obtain employment at certain restaurants or suppliers. The Retail Bakers of America (http://www.rbanet.com) offer certification for four levels of competence with a focus on several broad areas, including baking sanitation, management, retail sales, and staff training. The American Institute of Baking (http://www.aibonline.org) offers five career paths with certifications: certified baker, bread and sweet rolls; certified baker, cake and sweet goods; certified baker, cookies and crackers; certified ingredient service provider; and certified maintenance technician. In addition to baking skills and knowledge, bakers should have an eye for detail and good communication skills. Bakers may have direct reports if serving in a supervisory capacity. Some managerial positions may be available, or bakers may be promoted to a buyer position.

Executive Chef

An executive chef is not just a cook, he or she is usually totally in charge of the kitchen, which means keeping track of inventory and food supplies, preparing and designing menus, setting prices, and maybe even interviewing and hiring other kitchen staff members. Executive chefs are either classified as "working" or "nonworking." Working chefs prepare food alongside other chefs and cooks, nonworking executive chefs do not. This is a senior-level position. Most executive chefs have received formal education at colleges or culinary schools and have kitchen experience in other positions. Executive chefs can receive certification through the American Culinary

Federation, St. Augustine, Florida (http://www.acfchefs.org). Certification is not a requirement for the job. In addition to excellent kitchen skills, an executive chef should possess excellent communication, managerial, and basic business skills. All kitchen personnel typically report to the executive chef. This is the top of the line for most restaurants, as far as kitchen staff is concerned. However, some executive chefs may be promoted by being responsible for multiple locations of the same restaurant, or decide to become entrepreneurs and open their own restaurants.

Fast-Food Cook

Fast-food cooks work in chain or independent fast-food restaurants and prepare a limited selection of menu items. They cook and package batches of food, such as hamburgers, French fries, and fried chicken, to be kept warm until served. This is an entry-level position. Postsecondary education is not required, and in some cases a high school diploma is not required either. Most restaurants provide on-the-job training, which includes all aspects of food preparation, including food safety, sanitation, and workplace safety. Certifications are neither required nor available. Certifications are available to those who wish to learn more advanced cooking skills and are available through the American Culinary Federation. The OOH says cooks must be efficient, quick, and work well as part of a team. Manual dexterity is helpful for cutting, chopping, and plating. These workers also need creativity and a keen sense of taste and smell. Fast-food cooks do not have direct reports. Cooks who demonstrate an eagerness to learn new cooking skills and accept greater responsibility may also be asked to train or supervise less-skilled kitchen staff. Others may move to larger or more prestigious kitchens and restaurants, according to the OOH.

Fast-Food Shift Supervisor

Supervisors at fast-food establishments need to have the same knowledge and skill sets as their employees and may be required to cook or wait on customers in addition to supervising the employees during the shift. They are responsible for handling customer complaints and ensuring that food and service standards are met. This is a mid-level position. No postsecondary education is usually required. Instead most restaurants prefer experience in fast-food service along with proven supervisory or leadership skills. Most restaurants provide training. Certifications are not required to obtain employment, but depending on the direction the employee wants to take, he or she can become a certified food preparer or manager (see entries for Fast-Food Cook and Restaurant Manager for details). Supervisors should possess excellent communication skills and have the ability to handle high pressure and volume situations. All employees working a specific shift report to the supervisor. Shift supervisors can either be promoted to higher level kitchen duties or assistant manager or manager positions.

Garde Manger

In fine-dining and full-service restaurants the person serving in this position is responsible for creating salads, appetizers, and other small dishes that require minimum cooking or heating. Some employees in this position are required to create special designs with butter, cheese, and ice. Professionals in this position ensure that food is being served at the correct temperature and seasoned correctly. This is an entry-level position. Employers generally look for garde mangers that have completed culinary school or have years of experience serving under an executive chef. Garde mangers must be able to meet local requirements for food preparation. Certifications are not required to obtain employment, but are available through American Culinary Federation, St. Augustine, Florida (http://www.acfchefs .org). Garde mangers are expected to be creative and resourceful, have the ability to work as a team member, and have a strong work ethic. A garde manger does not have direct reports. In some restaurants garde mangers are considered sous chefs, but the typical career path for a garde manger is usually a promotion to chef, executive chef, or a position in a larger restaurant or kitchen.

Kitchen Manager

Similar to restaurant managers, kitchen managers are responsible for all kitchen operations, usually at independent full-service restaurants. They are responsible for maintaining inventories, keeping costs down, and recruiting, hiring, and managing kitchen staff and must have knowledge of food safety and health regulations. This is a mid-level position. No postsecondary education is usually required, although some fine-dining establishments prefer managers with culinary or hospitality degrees. Restaurants are looking for managers with previous kitchen management experience. Certifications are not required to obtain employment, but are available through the National Restaurant Association (http://www.restaurant.org). Certifications range from apprentice through master level. Restaurants also look for kitchen managers who have excellent communication, organizational, and leadership skills. All kitchen staff members report to the kitchen manager. In some fine-dining or full-service establishments kitchen managers can be promoted to general manager. In some chain restaurants kitchen managers can be promoted to larger restaurants or other managerial positions.

Kitchen Steward

The kitchen steward is responsible for the cleanliness of the kitchen and all the plate ware and utensils. His or her responsibilities include running and maintaining all cleaning equipment. This is an entry-level position. No postsecondary education is required. Certifications are neither required nor available. Some restaurants prefer previous experience but most are more concerned with an applicant's physical abilities. Employers are looking for kitchen stewards who can lift heavy objects (up to 150 pounds), stand on their feet for long periods of time, possess some mechanical aptitude, can work as part of a team, and can communicate in English. A steward does not have direct reports. If a steward is interested in learning other basic skills in a kitchen as an apprentice or trainee, he or she may advance to other positions in the kitchen.

Line/Prep Cook

Line cooks measure, mix, and cook ingredients according to recipes, using a variety of equipment, including pots, pans, cutlery, ovens, broilers, grills, slicers, grinders, and blenders. Line cooks may also be responsible for ordering food supplies and maintaining the smaller cooking equipment. In most cases this is considered an entry-level position, but in some kitchens it may be considered mid-level. No postsecondary education is usually required, although some full-service and fine-dining establishments prefer cooks with culinary degrees or previous experience in food service. Some restaurants provide training. Certifications are not required to obtain employment, but employees that want to become certified professional chefs can contact the American Culinary Federation, St. Augustine, Florida (http://www.acfchefs .org). Line cooks should genuinely enjoy working with food. Basic math and communication skills are also beneficial. A line cook does not have direct reports. The typical career path for a line cook is usually a promotion to chef, executive chef, or a position in a larger restaurant or kitchen.

Maitre d'hotel

This position is similar to restaurant manager and is more commonly available at hotels, cruise ships, and similar resorts. The maitre d'hotel is responsible for supervising food service staff and ensuring that all guests are experiencing the highest level of service and quality. They are in charge of reservations, seating, and other administrative tasks. This is a mid-level position. No postsecondary education is usually required, although some establishments require a minimum of one to two years of culinary school or other food service education, along with a minimum of three years experience in the field. Certifications are not required to obtain employment and are not offered for this specific position. The maitre d'hotel usually supervises the wait staff. The typical career path for this position is promotion into more mid-level management positions.

Pastry Chef

Pastry chefs focus on desserts and other baked items. They are required to produce great-tasting items while maintaining costs and inventory levels. They may be required to have advanced knife and culinary skills. They must be knowledgeable of kitchen and food safety procedures. This is a mid-level position. No postsecondary education is usually required, although most eating establishments prefer pastry chefs with formal culinary training and a minimum of two years of experience. Some restaurants provide training. Certifications are not required to obtain employment, but are available through the American Culinary Federation, St. Augustine, Florida (http://www .acfchefs.org). Pastry chefs are expected to conduct themselves in a professional manner. They must be detail-oriented and have a strong knowledge of kitchen and health requirements. Depending on the position and size of the kitchen, a pastry chef may have direct reports to assist him or her. The typical career path for a pastry chef is usually a promotion to head chef, executive chef, or a position in a larger restaurant or kitchen.

Short-Order Cook

Short-order cooks prepare foods and meals that do not require extensive preparation or cooking time. They must have the ability to cook and prepare food to order in a short amount of time, and possess basic kitchen skills and knowledge of food preparation and safety standards. This is an entry-level position. No postsecondary education is usually required, although some restaurants prefer short-order cooks with previous experience. Some restaurants provide training. Certifications are not required to obtain employment, but if short-order cooks are interested in becoming chefs, they can work toward certification through the American Culinary Federation, St. Augustine, Florida, (http://www.acfchefs.org). Short-order cooks are expected to possess basic math and communication skills, and the ability to work in high pressure or volume situations as part of a team. A short-order cook does not have direct reports. Unless the short-order cook aspires to the position of chef, advancement opportunities are limited.

Sommelier

The sommelier, or wine steward, is expected to have extensive knowledge of wines from all parts of the world. He or she must be able to suggest wines that are appropriate for the customers' meals or particular courses, and may manage wine inventory. This is considered a mid-level position. Most restaurants prefer sommeliers with formal training and education. Certifications are usually not required to obtain employment, but are available through the Court of Master Sommeliers (http://www.mastersommeliers.org), the American Sommelier Association (http://www.americansommelier.com), and the Sommelier Society of America (http://www.sommeliersocietyofamerica .org). Depending on the size of the restaurant, the sommelier may direct wine and/or bar servers. Sommeliers may become educators, trainers, or managers of larger establishments.

Sous Chef

Depending on the restaurant and how the kitchen is organized, sous chefs are typically the "right hand" of the executive chef. He or she is expected to work in some leadership, training, and supervisory capacities over line cooks and other kitchen staff members. He or she will also be responsible for performing the executive chef's job when the executive chef is not there. The sous chef may also assist the executive chef in menu preparation and monitoring food inventory levels. This is considered a mid-level position. Most restaurants prefer sous chefs with formal culinary training and education. Certifications are not required to obtain employment, but are available through the American Culinary Federation, St. Augustine, Florida (http://www .acfchefs.org). Sous chefs are expected to be creative, energetic, and have extensive cooking and knife skills. Sous chefs are also expected to have detailed knowledge of food safety and kitchen equipment and some leadership skills. Line cooks and other staff members may report to the sous chef. Sous chefs may me promoted to head chefs, executive chefs, or choose to open their own restaurants.

Restaurant: Front of House Staff

Bartenders

Bartenders are responsible for dispensing drinks to restaurant or bar patrons. Bartenders are required to know how to prepare mixed-drink orders, pour wines, beer, and dispense soft drinks and other beverages. Bartenders may also be responsible for serving diners in the bar area, and may be required to know the food menu and prepare the bill and collect payment. Bartending can be considered entry-level or mid-level depending on the position and type of facility. In a large restaurant or bar facility with a larger staff of bartenders, supervisory positions may be available. No formal education is required for bartenders, although bartending schools are available to teach formulas for drinks. Usually bartenders gain their expertise on the job. Certifications can be earned through various organizations and bartending schools, but are not a requirement for employment. A bartender usually does not have direct reports, but in a situation where there is a large bar staff, supervisory positions may be available. If bar staff supervisor positions are available this may be a career path. Otherwise, if the bartender is interested, he or she could learn kitchen duties or other front-of-house positions.

Busser

The busser is responsible for clearing tables after diners leave. It is his or her job to remove the dishes, silverware, etc. and reset the table as speedily as possible for quick turnaround of tables. He or she may also be responsible for keeping waiting staff stations stocked, or tables stocked with condiments. In some restaurants bussers will also expedite orders. This is an entry-level position. No postsecondary education is usually required. No certifications are required or offered. Bussers are required to possess the ability to stand for several hours and lift heavy objects. Bussers are also expected to have a friendly customer-service attitude and good communication skills. A busser does not have direct reports. There are no direct paths for promotion for bussers, although if the busser has expediting experience he or she may acquire a job as expediter.

Cashier

Cashiers work the point-of-sale (POS) registers and are responsible for properly inputting a customer's check, processing payments, and making change when necessary. Cashiers interact with customers and so must be friendly and professional. This is an entry-level position. No postsecondary education is usually required, although some employees prefer previous money-handling experience. Most restaurants provide training. Certifications are neither required nor offered. Cashiers are expected to possess basic math and communication skills, problem-solving skills, and the ability to work in a high pressure, fast-paced environment while accurately maintaining cash receipts. A cashier does not have direct reports. There are no typical or direct career paths for cashiers, although some may choose to advance to host or hostess positions or become part of the wait or serving staff where tips may be earned.

Expediter

Job descriptions of expediters vary from one restaurant to another. The expediter's duties may include making sure that each meal and dish is complete before the waiter or waitress takes it to the customer, including adding garnishes or condiments. Expediters may also serve as liaisons between wait staff and kitchen staff, responsible for advising wait staff when a menu item is out of stock or when special items are introduced. Expediters may also be required to stock wait stations. This is an entry-level position. No postsecondary education is usually required, although some food service operations prefer expediters with previous experience. Most restaurants provide training. Certifications are neither required nor offered. Expediters are expected to have good communication skills and the ability to work on their feet for long periods of time. Expediters should be friendly and enjoy working as part of a team. An expediter does not have direct reports. There are no direct career paths for expediters. If they have an interest they could apprentice in the kitchen or become a waiter or waitress.

Head Waiter/Waitress

Head waiters or waitresses provide the same service to customers as waiters or waitresses, but the supervisor or manager often assigns them other special duties. The head waiter or waitress may also be the first employee to deal with service complaints. This can be an entry-level position, but is most often considered mid-level. No postsecondary education is usually required, although some fine-dining establishments prefer head waiters or waitresses with culinary degrees. Some restaurants provide training. Certifications are not required to obtain employment, but are available through the Federation of Dining Room Professionals (http://www.fdrp.com). Certifications range from apprentice through master level. Head waiters or waitresses should genuinely enjoy working with people and striving for quality customer service. In many restaurants head waiters or waitresses are expected to have some knowledge of a dish's ingredients, and so must become familiar with the restaurant's menu. A head waiter or waitress does not have direct reports. In some fine-dining establishments employees interested in becoming members of kitchen staff, managers, or other more advanced positions are expected to start as members of the wait staff.

Host/Hostess

The responsibilities of the host or hostess may vary from restaurant to restaurant. Responsibilities can include seating guests; managing reservations; and providing guests with menus, high chairs, or other needed items. In some restaurants hosts also run the POS systems and are responsible for keeping any retail items stocked (if the restaurant sells take home items like baked goods, candy, gum, etc.). This is an entry-level position. No postsecondary education is usually required, although some food service operations prefer employees with previous experience. Most restaurants provide training. Certifications are not required to obtain employment, but are available through the Federation of Dining Room Professionals (http://www.fdrp.com). Certifications range from apprentice through master level. Hosts or hostesses should a genuinely enjoy working with people and striving for quality customer service. In many restaurants hosts or hostesses are expected to communicate any special menu items and do some suggestive selling. They may be required to have some knowledge of a dish's ingredients, and so must become familiar with the restaurant's menu. A host or hostess does not have direct reports. There are no direct career paths for hosts or hostesses.

Trainer

Some food service operations or large chains and corporations hire or promote personnel to train new hires or staff members that do not have kitchen or serving experience. The trainer is expected to communicate and teach new hires the methods and standards for preparing and serving food at the restaurants. They are also often required to teach food safety regulations and standards. This is a mid-level position. No postsecondary education is usually required, but trainers will need to have kitchen and food safety experience. Trainers will need to have certification in food safety. Certifications can be obtained through the National Restaurant Association's ServSafe program (http://www.restaurant.org) or through the National Registry of Foodservice Professionals. Some restaurants or food service operations will require trainers to have previous training experience. Trainers should have excellent communication and teaching skills, good organizational skills, and a desire for excellent customer service. A trainer does not have direct reports. Some large food service operations and corporations may have larger training departments, and trainers could advance to supervisory or management positions.

Waiters/Waitresses

Waiters and waitresses, also called servers, are front-of-house employees who take customers' orders; they usually deliver meals to the tables as well. Servers are responsible for taking care of all of a restaurant customer's needs from beverages to dessert. This is an entry-level position. No postsecondary education is usually required, although some fine-dining establishments prefer servers with culinary degrees. Some restaurants provide training. Certifications are not required to obtain employment, but are available through the Federation of Dining Room Professionals (http://www.fdrp.com). Certifications range from apprentice through master level. Servers should genuinely enjoy working with people and striving for quality customer service. In many restaurants servers are expected to have some knowledge of the menu so they can answer guests' questions. A server does not have direct reports. In some fine-dining establishments employees interested in becoming members of kitchen staff, managers, or other more advanced positions are expected to start as servers.

Non-Restaurant Positions

Cafeteria Cook

Cafeteria cooks typically work in noncommercial food service establishments or in the cafeterias of businesses, hospitals, schools, or prisons. Like cooks at commercial food service operations, cafeteria cooks are expected to prepare meats, vegetables, and other foods for customer consumption. Depending on the location, cafeteria cooks may be required to cook to higher nutritional standards. This is an entry-level position. No postsecondary education is usually required, although some food service operations prefer cooks with previous experience. Some operations provide training. Certifications are not required to obtain employment, but certifications in food safety would be considered a plus. Cooks must have the ability and skills to prepare and serve meals. They must have good communication skills and be able to stand for long periods of time. A cafeteria cook usually does not have direct reports. Depending on the size of the operation some cooks may be promoted to head cook or kitchen manager.

Caterer

Caterers are usually independent or self-employed but some are hired by food service companies or restaurants to cater functions for business or other clients. Caterers work with clients to prepare a menu for a specific function, whether it is a business luncheon or an anniversary party. Customers typically pay per meal and caterers prepare

Best
Practice
Choosing the Right Job

How do you know what career and job will work for you? As in most things in life, there are no guarantees you will love your job or career. Two ways to determine whether you will like a job is to talk to others that are doing the job now, and actually try the job out. When you talk to the person actually doing the job find out if you can job shadow him or her for a day or two. That can give you a great idea of what the job is actually like. There are also several books and Web sites where you can take quizzes and evaluate your skills and interests in order to determine a career choice best suited for you. Examples are *Career Tests: 25 Revealing Self-Tests to Help You Find and Succeed at the Perfect Career* by Louis H. Janda, (Free-Career-Test.com), and (LiveCareer.com).

and deliver the food to the client's location. This is a mid-level position. No postsecondary education is usually required, although most operations prefer caterers with a culinary degree or food services or catering experience. People interested in becoming caterers or starting a catering business can earn a certificate through some culinary schools or become a certified catering executive through the National Association of Catering Executives (http://www.nace.net). Some restaurants provide training. Caterers are expected to have a valid driver's license and a friendly, customer-service oriented attitude. A caterer does not have direct reports. Depending on the size and type of the organization, sales or management positions may be available.

Cookbook Writer/Editor

Cookbook writers develop creative or innovative ideas for cookbooks, compile or develop recipes, and write them in a cohesive and enjoyable format. Editors that specialize in cookbooks usually have a culinary background, understand cooking preparation techniques, and pocess basic editing skills. This is a mid-level position. A college degree in

English, journalism, or communications is usually preferred for editors, and formal training or experience in the culinary industry is preferred for both writers and editors. There are usually no direct reports for these positions. Writers may be promoted to editors, and editors may be promoted to managing editors or publishers.

Customer Service/Manager

Customer service or food service managers are typically employed at grocery stores, convenience stores, gas stations, etc. in the food service area of the store. They are required to provide customer service in the area. Managers are required to manage the food service area by making sure supplies are stocked and customers are receiving quality customer service. There are positions available at all levels. No postsecondary education is usually required, although some companies prefer employees with previous experience. Most companies provide training. Certifications are neither required nor available. Customer service providers or managers should have excellent communication, organizational, and customer service skills. A manager will have customer service representatives reporting to him or her. Depending on the size of the company, other management positions may be available.

Dietician/Nutritionist

Dieticians and nutritionists are primarily employed by hospitals or other health care organizations, although fitness facilities and similar organizations also hire dieticians to develop menus. Dieticians look at patients' medical diagnoses and laboratory levels and create diets for patients to follow while at the hospital or under medical care. Nutritionists perform similar work. This is a mid-level position. Dieticians and nutritionists must have bachelor's degrees and valid licenses for the state in which they work. Most employers seek experienced dieticians. Although not required, the Commission on Dietetic Registration of the American Dietetic Association (http://www.eatright.org) awards the Registered Dietitian credential to those who pass an exam after completing academic course work and a supervised internship. Dieticians and nutritionists are expected to have good communication and organizational skills. A nutritionist or dietician does not have direct reports. Experienced dietitians may become self-employed or advance to management positions, such as assistant director, associate director, or director of a dietetic department.

District Manager

District managers are responsible for managing the operations of several restaurant units within a geographic area. They are responsible for ensuring that sales goals are achieved as well as all other budget goals, such as cost containment. They ensure customers' satisfaction and fair administration of regional personnel policies, procedures, and guidelines. This is a high level position. A bachelor's degree and 5 to 10 years of experience in the food service industry are required. Some operations may require the employee to have previous multi-unit management experience. Certifications are not required but are available through the International Food Service Executives Association (http://www.ifsea.com). The certified Foodservice Management Professional (FMP) designation is earned through the National Restaurant Association (http://www.restaurant.org). District managers are expected to have strong financial, analytical, and leadership skills. A district manager will have several direct reports, usually an administrative assistant, and unit restaurant managers. District managers may advance to other executive positions within their organization.

Food Critic

Food critics may be independent reviewers, or they may be hired by particular publications to visit restaurants and write full reviews of the quality of the food and service. This is considered a mid-level position. A college degree in English, communications, or journalism, combined with formal culinary training, is usually the required or preferred level of education for this position. Food critics should have a passion for food, knowledge of the industry, and excellent writing skills. Certifications are not required to obtain employment. Some people use culinary certifications to become critics. There are no direct reports for this position. Critics may find employment with larger publications with a wider audience.

Food Writer/Editor

Food writers or editors are typically employed by a particular publication and write about trends in the industry. Full-time and freelance positions are usually available. There are positions available at all levels. A college degree is required, usually in writing related fields like English, journalism, or communications. Certifications are not required to obtain employment and are not available. Both writers and editors should have excellent writing skills, an excellent command of the English language, and good organizational skills. Editors in charge of writers also need to have supervisory and people skills. Food writers and editors should also have experience and knowledge of the industry. A culinary background is helpful. An editor may have writers reporting to him or her. Depending on the size of the publication, management positions may be available.

Personal Chef

There are two types of personal chefs. Personal chefs may be hired exclusively by one household to prepare all meals served there each day. A more common type of personal chef is an independent chef who prepares and sells meals for several different clients. Sometimes the personal chef prepares the meals in the client's kitchen. Other times he or she prepares them off-site and delivers them to the clients. This second type of personal chef is most often an independent operator, and not an employee. This is an entry-level position. Most clients hiring personal chefs, whether as an employee or for occasional meals, prefer chefs with culinary backgrounds and food service experience. Certifications are not required but are available through the United States Personal Chef Association (http://www .uspca.com). Personal chefs should enjoy planning and preparing meals of all kinds, customized to meet the needs of their clients, and have good communication and customer service skills. Depending on the chef's clientele or specialty, some culinary training and knowledge of nutritional needs may be required. A personal chef does not have direct reports unless he or she has a large business and hired employees to assist him or her. Depending on the size of the household or business the personal chef is hired by, promotions may be available for supervisory positions. Personal chefs may also be hired as chefs at food service operations.

Project Manager

Project managers are most often hired by non-restaurant food service organizations such as school and business food service organizations and food service suppliers. Project managers are responsible for leading a project team and ensuring each project goal is met by its deadline. Projects include the incorporation of new technologies, concepts, locations, and menu items. This is a mid-level position. A bachelor's degree and some experience in project management and food service are usually required. Certifications are not required but are available through the Project Management Institute (http://www.pmi.org). Entry-level project managers will work with more experienced managers until they have gained more experience. Project managers are expected to be assertive, flexible, and have good communication skills. A project manager usually does not have direct reports. Depending on the size of the organization, supervisory and management positions may be available.

Retail Manager

Retail managers are hired by contract food service operations in businesses, schools, or hospital cafeteria settings to manage the operations of these businesses. Retail managers are responsible for the successful retail/cafeteria operations usually under the guidance of the director. Retail managers perform a variety of duties, including the planning and supervision of special functions, maintaining cash controls, payroll records, and hiring and training of hourly team members. The retail manager ensures customer satisfaction and good public relations through the safe and efficient use of resources. This is a mid-level position. A bachelor's degree is required along with three to five years of experience in the industry, usually in a management role. Certifications are not required but are available through National Restaurant Association (http://www.restaurant.org). Retail managers should have knowledge of food and catering trends with a focus on quality, production, sanitation, food cost controls, and marketing and presentation. They are also expected to possess supervisory, leadership, management, and coaching skills as well as good communication skills, both written and verbal. Retail managers should be knowledgeable of financial, budgetary, accounting, and computational practices. Staff members at a retail location will report to the retail manager. Depending on the size of the company, additional managerial and executive positions may be available.

Chapter 4

Tips for Success

No one said it would be easy. The food services industry is full of oxymorons. It is glamorous and grueling, rewarding and thankless, enjoyable and terribly challenging. Few industries can push and develop someone like food services. Employees work long hours, often constantly on their feet, and must face countless customers with smiles on their faces. But it is undeniable that something about it gets into the blood. That is why Jim Grote, founder and CEO of Donatos Pizza, recommends that anyone choosing a career in this industry *must* have a passion for it in order to succeed. "Do something you love," he says. "I was and continue to be passionate about great-tasting pizza and providing excellent customer service. If you do something you love, then it doesn't feel like work."

Launching a career in this industry means working at a restaurant or other food service outlet, a supplier, consulting firm, or starting a restaurant. In any of these situations, the person must be willing to do what it takes to survive and succeed.

Getting a Job

It used to be that looking for a job meant hours scouring the want ads in newspapers. Those days are long gone. Today there are a wide range of job boards and Web sites where job seekers can search for their dream jobs. Most employers post openings on one or several sites, which can then be re-posted at other sites. If you do not have Internet access at home, it is a good idea to go to the library at least a few times a week to check for new job postings. Karen Ickes, senior vice president of human resources with Wendy's International, says job seekers must use the Internet to find work today.

There are the major job Web sites as well as sites specific to food service industry jobs. If you are looking for a job at a specific company, postings may also be on the company's Web site, like Wendy's. Clint R. Lautenschleger, director of staffing at Bob Evans Farms, Inc., agrees that for entry-level and corporate jobs, checking ads on Web sites is the best way to go. "As with most of the service and hospitality industry, online job boards such as CareerBuilder and Monster are the most popular and prevalent sources for posting open positions," he says. "Due to the wide variety in companies represented in these industries it is also beneficial to constantly review company Web sites."

Some of the most frequently visited job Web sites today are Yahoo! HotJobs, JobCentral.com, CollegeRecruiter.com, CareerBuilder.com, Monster.com, Job.com, Career.com, TrueCareers.com, Indeed.com, Net-Temps.com, and Craigslist.org.

Web sites that are devoted to the food services industry and post open positions include Hospitality Works, Resources in Food, Foodservice.com, Foodservicecareers.com, and RestaurantJobsNetwork. com. Another great way to find jobs is through industry associations. If you are a member of an association check that association's Web site. Chances are jobs are posted somewhere on the site, and there could be advantages to looking for jobs through an association. Often job boards are only open to association members, and jobs are not posted at traditional job boards, so you are competing with a much smaller pool of people.

Lautenschleger cautions that Web sites are not the best way to obtain *every* job. "As you migrate up the hierarchy into field management one should understand the company culture and how you obtain such a position," he says. "Some companies offer only internal promotion while others may use third-party recruiting agencies to fill these field management positions. The most effective way to know the answer to this is to check with the company firsthand."

Finally, a great way to find open positions is through word of mouth. Just ask. If you have a friend that works at the company that you are interested in, give him or her a call and ask if there are any openings. Even if there are not openings at the time of your call, you have planted a seed in your friend's mind, so that when an opening pops up your friend will think of you.

In fact, many experts agree that networking is the number one way to find a job today. According to Ickes, companies are flooded with résumés for every position they advertise. Networking is a way to stand out from the crowd, which is extremely important. Ickes recommends reaching out to previous coworkers when networking. She says to indicate that you are exploring new opportunities.

Lautenschleger agrees. "Networking with individuals at a company remains yet another increasingly effective way to land a future position. In general, hiring managers have a certain comfort level in really knowing a candidate—beyond what they learn during an interview—and personal referrals can go a long way in increasing your chances."

Today networking is not just accomplished through traditional means and relationships. Networking is also done through social Web sites such as Facebook, Twitter, and LinkedIn. As your network and interests broaden you will find others with the same interests and connections to more people in the industry. New opportunities may come your way when you are not even looking.

Once you have applied to some jobs and landed an interview the best policy is always to be honest about your goals, objectives, skills, and salary requirements. Like any good relationship, you are bound to find yourself mismatched with a job or company if you are not honest about what you are looking for.

Dr. Randall S. Hansen is founder of Quintessential Careers, one of the oldest and most comprehensive career development sites on the Internet. He is also CEO of EmpoweringSites.com. He has put together a list of dos and don'ts when it comes to job interviews. While some of these may seem like common sense, it is surprising how many people make these faux pas. Among his list of dos: Do brush your teeth or pop a breath mint before the interview. Do travel to the interview location prior to the day of the interview so you are familiar with how to get there and how long it takes to do so. Do stress your accomplishments and dress appropriately. Do shake hands firmly, wait until you are asked to be seated, and avoid using poor language and pause words such as "um" and "uh." Do ask intelligent questions about the company and at the end of the interview do tell the interviewer you want the job and ask about the next step in the process.

His list of don'ts includes: Don't chew gum during the interview. Don't bring up controversial topics. Don't speak negatively of previous bosses, companies, or coworkers. Don't smoke, even if the interviewer does and offers you a cigarette. Don't tell jokes during the interview, and don't appear desperate for the job. Don't answer any question with a single yes or no answer; instead, give an explanation for your answer as much as possible. Finally, always be honest.

Building a Professional Reputation

Once you have obtained your dream job—or the closest thing to it—in the very competitive food services industry, you will be concerned about building a professional reputation. Most human resource professionals advise employees to look at both their external customers and their internal customers when building a reputation. Your external customers are those outside of the company. They include not only the restaurant's customers, but also those you do business with outside the restaurant, such as bankers, printers, and accountants. That is why it is important to conduct yourself professionally at all times.

Another way to build a professional reputation outside your company is to get involved in a professional organization, says Ickes. "Build an external network," she says. "Go to seminars and conferences and if you've participated in a unique project share your findings with your peers there."

Inside the organization you need to become the "go-to" person others will think of when opportunities arise. "Know as much as you can about as much as you can," Lautenschleger recommends. "But don't lose sight of what your core duties are. Building relationships internally will assist with this, and it makes you invaluable if tough times ever do come around."

Ickes recommends establishing relationships with your peers within your organization. Get to know the people you work with in other departments. "Opportunities arise when you build upon your knowledge base and get to know your peers," she says.

There is no getting around the fact that the food services industry focuses on people and relationships, perhaps more so than any other industry today. In order for an up and coming employee to create the most professional reputation possible, it is essential to have excellent communication skills, listen to your internal and external clients, and know how to respond when the feedback is less than positive. Here are some tips to keep in mind when building a professional reputation.

Tip #1: Use active listening techniques. Often in the food services industry, things just do not go as planned. The results can be unhappy customers and employees. Managers and supervisors are usually the ones to listen to their complaints and problems. Although not every problem can be easily solved, sometimes the best results occur when the customer or employee knows he or she is being heard and understood. That is where active listening comes in. If possible, take the customer or employee to a quiet location where he or she can be clearly heard. Next, listen and focus on what the person is saying. Do not interrupt or form responses while the person is speaking. Wait patiently for him or her to finish his or her thought. Finally, sum up what the person said when responding before proposing a solution to the problem. That way the person knows he or she has been heard and understood. This can go a very long way to defusing the tension in the situation.

Tip #2: Stay positive when on the job site. As mentioned, this industry is one where anything and everything can go wrong at the drop of a hat. While the temptation may exist to voice disappointment, anger, and other negative emotions, this will most likely not fix the situation. In fact, it can affect others on the team in a negative way. It certainly will not create a professional reputation. Instead, voice concerns with employees, customers, and managers in a way that is positive and approaches the situation from a problem-solving standpoint. For example, there may be an irate customer who is complaining a great deal. Instead of discussing it with the manager in terms of, "Man, all this customer does is gripe and complain," a better way to phrase it would be, "This customer has a lot of complaints. What can we do to address them?" It describes the situation accurately, but without being negative or judgmental.

Tip #3: Do not talk negatively about other employees or customers. Food service industry professionals meet and work with a wide range of people, from sales people, bankers, wholesalers, and suppliers to chefs, important customers, and food critics. It is important to create a professional reputation by keeping conversations as positive as possible, no matter how unpleasant the situation may be. That includes not making snide remarks about the boss and co-workers. At the end of the day, at home and away from the company, feel free to vent emotions to close friends and family members who will not spread the words. When on the job, refrain from doing so, no matter how tempting it might be. Grumbling to a co-worker about the manager may seem like an okay thing to do at the time,

Keeping
in Touch

You just concluded a great interview for your dream job. Do you send a thank you note?

Absolutely, says Karen Ickes, senior vice president of human resources for Wendy's International. "A quick hand-written thank you note is the most personal," she says. While you may be tempted to take the easy route and send your note via e-mail, if the position is really important to you, fight that temptation. "Many candidates simply run home and send a pre-written e-mail thank you note," says Clint R. Lautenschleger, director of staffing at Bob Evans Farms, Inc. "That is fine, but to make a real impression take the time to hand write a note. It seems simple, but it is not done as much anymore. You will be remembered."

Ickes says it is OK to make an additional salient point in relation to the job, but do not use the note as a sales tool, because that can turn people off.

And always send your note 24 to 48 hours following the interview. "The interviewer should receive it within a week," Ickes says.

but that co-worker may end up becoming the boss and remember that conversation. Or the co-worker may decide to tell the boss about the conversation if an opportunity presents itself. Negative conversations often have a way of coming back to haunt the participants, so the best policy is just not to have them.

Tip #4: Have a team approach. In this industry, each person depends on *someone* for *something*. The wait staff depends on the kitchen staff to properly prepare the food. The chefs depend on the kitchen managers to order high quality ingredients. In order for the operation to be a success, each person must also be successful, which can only occur when employees work together as a team. Remember the most delicious meal ever prepared may not be worth a repeat visit to the restaurant if it was sloppily served on dirty dishes. Likewise, the best service in town cannot overcome inedible food. Take a team approach each day on the job. Observe what others need to be successful and do what it takes to ensure this success. Other team members will notice and the team spirit will spread, creating a well-coordinated operation and happy customers.

▼

Tip #5: There is no such thing as too much communication. The menu was discussed at the server meeting. Memos were written and distributed. Everyone should know the details of the upcoming event, shouldn't they? What about the person who was sick and could not attend the meeting and did not get the memo? In a business that is very detail-intense, communication is crucial for making sure that everyone has the information they need to do their jobs. This includes having meetings, asking questions, putting things in writing, and never assuming *anything*. Creating and distributing checklists and conducting one final meeting before a large event or function can prevent small issues or big disasters from occurring. Make sure information is communicated first-hand, not through a secondary source, and reiterate important details. Communicate expectations as well.

How to Get Promoted

Some people think the best way to earn a promotion is by earning an MBA. Others say the best way is to find a mentor within the organization who can offer you advice and support. While neither of these methods is going to hurt your chances of getting promoted, they certainly are not going to get you there exclusively. Sandy J. Wayne, professor and director of the Center for Human Resource Management at the University of Illinois, Chicago, conducted a study of 570 employees and 289 managers at a large company in the United States. She asked them to rank the most important factors influencing promotions. The results were surprising. What the employees thought would earn them promotions was very different than the factors cited by managers. For the employees, having an MBA from a highly ranked school ranked at the top of the list. Their bosses cited leadership skills as the most important factor. Employees also gave a high rank to having a mentor. Executives hardly mentioned this at all. They were looking for employees with a strong work ethic.

The fact is there is no magic bullet or formula that will ensure a promotion, but there are things you can do that can improve your chances and keep you in mind so when opportunities come up you will make the list of those considered. Both Ickes and Lautenschleger agree that you can forget any chances of promotion if you are not competent in your current position. "It is certainly important to be extremely competent in your current role," says Ickes. "You must be meeting your goals and objectives." Lautenschleger takes this a step further, saying you will not even be considered unless you have proven yourself competent in your present position. Once it is clear you have mastered your current level, there are actions you can take and things to avoid that will increase your chances of getting a promotion. Lautenschleger advises employees to look at the job you would like and the skills it requires. Most likely there will be skill sets that you either do not have, or have not been able to prove that you have. Lautenschleger says managers are more likely to promote employees that take the initiative to acquire the skills that appear to be missing.

"Remember that the job you want likely requires very different skills and unless you are working in a large organization with many developmental programs in place you may have to self-develop," he says. "Example being, if you are a great specialist but want to be the manager of the specialists you not only have to be a great specialist, but also show you can be a great leader. This must be accomplished by both formal and informal means. Show the decision makers you are willing to take on leadership assignments and prove you are willing to invest in yourself through training, reading, and education."

Ickes recommends getting involved in other activities at the company. Volunteer to help out, organize, and lead projects and community work. You will be demonstrating to managers that you can supervise and lead others. Ickes also recommends working with the current supervisor to develop a strategy that will lead to the job the employee is eying. It is also a good idea to find a mentor in the department to which the employee wants to be promoted. Remember not to rely on mentoring alone. Mentoring will only work if you have proven yourself capable in your current position and are working to prove you have the skills required to move to the next level.

Marian R. Ruderman and Patricia J. Ohlott (*Standing at the Crossroads: Next Steps for High-Achieving Women*) looked at why promotions occurred at three Fortune 500 companies. They looked at 61 promotions that were considered typical at the companies and asked what had led to the promotions. Their research indicates that the promotions were based on the individuals' efforts and abilities. They found that jobs were often created to fit the candidate. The decision makers did not place much emphasis on formal assessments, such as performance evaluations. They found that in almost half of the cases, only one person was considered for the job. In addition, a tremendous variety existed among the types of promotions. The bottom line of the research was that organizational context should be considered when trying to understand promotions. In other words, spend time

Problem
Solving

How to Decline a Job You Do Not Want

It may not happen often, but the delightful dilemma of receiving two job offers does happen. Which one should you choose? Unless the offers are nearly identical, which is highly unlikely, you probably already know which one you want, says Karen Ickes, Wendy's International senior vice president of human resources. What if you receive one offer, and are waiting for a second? Ickes says to be honest with the company who has already tendered the offer. "Tell the company you need more time to contemplate the offer," she says. "You can usually ask for about a week." She says if the company is pressed for time and needs an answer sooner it does not hurt to let the person know you are interviewing elsewhere. In fact, she says, if the company that presented the offer knows that, they may make their offer more attractive. "It certainly heightens a company's interest in you," Ickes says. "But don't lie about it, if that is not the case."

Once you have decided which job you are choosing make sure you are gracious when declining the other offer, and do give a reason for your decision. "Explain the logic for your decision," says Clint Lautenschleger, of Bob Evans Farms, Inc. "The hiring manager or recruiter may not want to hear it, but you owe it to them to explain why you made your decision. They hopefully would reciprocate if they chose a different candidate for a position."

to really understand the company's culture and the process used to hire and promote. Each company will be different. Ask questions and do your research.

Elizabeth Freedman, MBA, is an award-winning speaker and business columnist, and is the author of *Work 101: Learning the Ropes of the Workplace without Hanging Yourself* and *The MBA Student's Job-Seeking Bible*. She offers some dos and don'ts when it comes to seeking promotions. Among her dos are: Do imitate those who have the job you want. She advises people to take them out to coffee or lunch and ask questions about what qualities have made them successful on the job. Do become an expert in your field. She encourages workers to join industry associations and groups and attend their meetings and seminars even if you have to pay for them yourself. She says that the education and networking you will experience will be worth every penny of the investment and make you more marketable to your company and others.

Another important item in Freedman's list is to understand your boss and his or her priorities. When you see how your job fits in with your boss's and prioritize your work in conjunction with his or hers you make your boss look good. And in turn you will look good. It will also help you to understand when the best time is to ask questions or when he or she needs to be left alone. These kinds of considerations go a long way.

Another point Freedman makes is that employees need to make an effort to get along with all coworkers no matter how old they are. This is especially true in the food services industry, where coworkers can be anywhere from 16 to 65. We all tend to gravitate toward people our own age or think of younger people as our kids or older people as our parents. But when you work with people of different age ranges it is important to put those tendencies aside and find common ground. A food service staff has to work together as a team if it is going to function smoothly and for the success of all involved. So remember that you are all on the same team and try to get along.

Just as important, says Freedman are some pretty clear don'ts. One of her top don'ts is trying to fight the current system. Even if you clearly see some of its inefficiencies, the best way to correct them is working with the system rather than against it. Making suggestions for improvements is a positive way to initiate needed changes. Remember where you are in the hierarchy and work within the scope of your position as you try to make things more efficient.

Another don't Freedman has seen at different companies is forgetting that you and your work are always visible. It may seem sometimes like no one is paying attention or a particular task is not important, but performing sloppily will always come back to haunt you. It may also be that the task you thought no one cared about was the one task management is watching to determine if you are manager material. Always perform at your best and view every project as an opportunity to show your stuff.

Another sure way to stifle your chances of promotion, says Freedman, is to get the reputation as a complainer. You may be entirely correct about the problems within the organization, but if you take every opportunity to complain about them rather than taking a more positive approach, you will be seen as the complainer instead of the person with great ideas for improvement. Freedman says you might also be seen as someone who is not knowledgeable enough about the company or the industry to know what works and what does not. The best way to proceed when things just are not "right" in your eyes is to do your research, ask questions, and make suggestions to decision makers. Keep your complaints private.

Lastly, don't become invisible, says Freedman. You may be overwhelmed with work, but if you bury yourself and do not volunteer to help others or make a real effort to connect with coworkers on a regular basis your name will not be one of the first mentioned when an opportunity comes along.

Planning Your Career

Like getting a promotion, there is no one way to plan your career in the food services industry or any other industry. Experts agree that the bottom line is you have to know what you really want, and then work with key people to develop a plan to get it.

"You must first identify what you want," Bob Evans' Lautenschleger says. For some that may be the easy part. For others it is not so easy. Freedman says there have been numerous cases of people spending years pursuing a specific career only to land that dream job and realize it was not what they thought it was at all. Before you find yourself in that position, if you have not already done so, spend some time in the area of the industry you have chosen. Talk to people who are already where you want to be and ask them lots of questions. Make sure the career path you are choosing is really going to give you the end results you're looking for.

Ickes says you definitely have to have self-awareness and initiative when planning your career and know exactly what it is you want.

Once you have determined what you want, then what? How do you go about realizing your dreams? Lautenschleger says to make sure your goals are realistic. "Not everyone can be the CEO, but perhaps the director or VP is a more suitable role for a particular person or skill level," he says. Then, depending on your ultimate goal and your current position, you have a few options. If you are employed by a larger company with a human resources department, you can meet with a professional in that department, to discuss your career goals and develop a career plan. "HR professionals can help

Professional Ethics

Should You Exaggerate During an Interview?

While this may sound like a no-brainer at first glance, what we actually do in a pressure situation when we really need and want a job may be a different matter. Many people have been known to lie or exaggerate about their skills in an interview situation. And both human resource professionals Clint Lautenschleger and Karen Ickes say that is not okay. Not only will it almost always be discovered that you lied, but it could also mean immediate dismissal from the position.

"Any savvy recruiter or hiring manager will eventually perform reference checks and will eventually learn about your 'little white lie,'" says Lautenschleger. "You are much better off being truthful about your experiences. A great rule of thumb is the less you exaggerate, the less you have to remember to what extent you exaggerated. Tell the truth and your story is always the same!" Remember, says Ickes, falsifying information on an application is grounds for termination.

you develop a plan," Ickes says. "But remember the individual is responsible and accountable for making it happen."

Just as you did when working toward a promotion, look at the skills required for your ultimate goal and then at the skills you currently possess. If you are missing some basic skills take it upon yourself to develop them, either through your company and the training it has to offer, or through other educational opportunities like college courses and continuing education through industry associations. It is also important to continue to stay in touch with industry trends, company culture, and opportunities inside and outside your current scope of responsibilities. You will be more likely to reach your ultimate goal, enjoy it, and succeed if you do.

Continuing Education and Certifications

It seems these days that just about every job in every profession offers some certification and continuing education requirements, and the food services industry is no exception. While most jobs do not require certifications, they do not hurt and can give you a competitive edge over those who do not hold certifications. Of course some jobs do require a certain educational background or certification. For example if you were looking for a position as a chef, most employers want to see that you have attended a culinary school. "Clearly someone with interest in the food industry—particularly in the realm of chef— needs to attend some sort of formal culinary training," notes Lautenschleger. "For management, it is not quite as clear cut. Take advantage of whatever courses your company offers, but also look toward your local college or university for leadership and/or business classes or even certification programs."

In Chapter 3, "On the Job," you will find a listing of jobs in the industry, and in each listing you will see whether there is specific education or certifications offered or required. Generally speaking, most employees in the industry can get certifications related to their field through an industry association. For example, if you are a public relations coordinator for a large restaurant chain, you can get certification through the Public Relations Society of America. Certain professions, like IT professionals, must be certified in certain software and management programs to land particular jobs. Before you take the time and spend the money to earn a certification, talk to managers and HR professionals to make sure it will truly benefit you.

Tess Price has a Ph.D. in human resources organizational development and adult education and is a columnist for Office Arrow, a professional development Web site for administrators. Price says certifications can mean the difference in whether you are considered or hired for a particular job. "If you are certified in your job area but another applicant is not, you may improve your chances of getting an interview or being hired," says Price. In fact, she adds that it may actually be a satisfactory substitute for postsecondary education in some fields. To determine whether you need certification and continuing education, it is always best to rely on your human resources professional and the culture in your company.

Advice for Chefs and Restaurant Entrepreneurs

While all the advice given so far could be applied to employees in various food services operations, what about those who are pursuing excellence as a chef or starting their own restaurants? These fields attract many creative and talented people, but it takes more than just talent to succeed in this very tough industry.

As a culinary arts professional, it is a matter of providing consistent, quality products, and less about proving you are better than someone else. One chef who can speak that message from experience is Chef Dave Martin, teacher and chef at New York City's Vynl restaurants. He is most well-known as a season one contestant on Bravo TV Network's *Top Chef* and he says not to let your ego get in the way. "You really cannot have an ego in this business," Martin says. "The word 'passion' gets used a lot, maybe it is overused, but it is not a glamorous job. You really have to love it." Martin says he left a lucrative career because of his love of creating delicious foods. "But you have to be hard-working. You still have to have some blue collar in you. There will be times when you need to wash dishes, bus tables, whatever it takes to get the job done." Martin says not only may you have to help out in these capacities, but that it is also very beneficial for you to do so. "You have to understand what it is like to be a waiter or a bus boy," he says. "You are part of a team and that's really important to appreciate and understand what it takes to get it all done."

Martin says it is important to work together as a team because your recipes will not be consistent if your team of cooks does not respect you. "I can go in and re-create recipes, but if no one is overseeing me I can turn them into whatever I want. As a chef I need to be personable and earn respect. They will not make the food the way I want them to if they don't respect me."

Martin says it is hard to find that middle ground between being nice and being the boss. "You have to be nice, but you also have to be someone who inspires people and who they can learn from and respect on all levels," he says. "That's where you have to lose the ego and attitude. For goodness sake you're cooking dinner for people. Know the customer and be about the customer. Leave the ego thing behind. We're all in this business to make people happy."

Finally, Martin says, be prepared to start at the bottom, and not for a lot of money. "You really need to think it through," he says. "It's a hard road and you'll work for some tough chefs. Not every chef is nice. Be prepared. It can be great, but it's hard work. You have to suck it up and just keep going."

Victor Gielisse, associate vice president at the Culinary Institute of America, advises new chefs to learn about global flavor. "Ethnic cuisines used to be pretty broadly defined," he says. "Food was labeled Asian, Latin, or Mediterranean. As it became more popular it also became more regional. Today we have South American, Sicilian, and Indonesian. We're seeing a global palette of more authentic

INTERVIEW

Career Advice from a Human Resources Professional

Karen Ickes
Senior vice president of human resources for Wendy's International

What are the best ways for someone to get a job in the food services industry today?
Today the best way to find a job is using Internet job boards. Stay on top of the sites that employers are using for your field. For example, research and development and marketing departments lean toward sites more oriented toward those fields. Networking is certainly important. With the unemployment rate as high as it is [in summer 2009], when a job is advertised we are flooded with applicants. It is hard to stand out in the crowd. If you know someone you have worked with, a boss, etc., contact him or her and let that person know you are exploring new opportunities.

What are the best strategies for building a professional reputation?
The best strategy for building a professional reputation is to get involved in a professional organization. You will get to know others outside your company and build an external network. Also, attending or speaking at seminars and conferences, and sharing findings of new, unique projects will build your reputation. Within [an] organization, [you need to] establish relationships. If you work with the accounting department, get to know your peers there. Build upon that relationship and volunteer to participate in initiatives and opportunities available. That will build your knowledge base and you will get to know your peers.

What are some good strategies for getting promoted?
Certainly it is important to be extremely competent in your current role. Meet all of your goals and objectives and get involved in other activities. Work with your supervisor to build a strategy for promotion. Ask him or her for help in putting together a development plan. Also, find a mentor in the department to which you would like to move.

foods. We have our own cuisines but chefs everywhere are learning these." Gielisse says this trend is also due to the fact that people are more well-read and educated thanks to televised cooking shows.

Gielisse also stresses the importance of getting and maintaining an education. "The education students receive today is unbelievable," he says. "They are immersed in histories and cultures. Creativity comes later. But it is never-ending. You have to take a path of continual education. You have to be current and stay abreast of things through classes, blogs, Twitter, [or] another course or program."

Gielisse says it is not enough to just stay on top of trends; it is also important to find ways to bring extra value to an organization. "Technically you can be capable, but you also need to pursue personal growth. And you have to maintain a professional profile even when it is difficult. That can be the biggest differentiator in the business."

Operation: Success

If launching your career in the industry means that you are looking to start your own restaurant, you are not alone. Starting any new business, especially one as challenging as a restaurant, can be an extremely daunting task. Longtime veterans and industry experts provide some solid advice for new entrepreneurs.

Francine Cohen, editor in chief of *Food & Beverage Magazine*, says the primary driver of any operation has to be quality. "Over the last two or three years it has become more evident that quality is the primary driver over quantity," she says. "Menu engineering is all about providing quality food and service at a decent price point."

Jin Grote, founder and CEO of Donatos Pizza, has been in the business for 45 years. He agrees with Cohen. "Customers' desire for great-tasting food that is consistent will never change. And neither will the need to provide outstanding service to create loyal customers who return to your restaurant again and again."

Chef Dave Martin says the importance of the location you choose for your restaurant cannot be overemphasized. "You have to aware of the demographics in the area. You cannot go into an area where there are a large number of Chinese residents and open a Latin American restaurant. You have to look at the neighborhood."

Mario Ponce, a restaurant consultant and principal of Partners in Hospitality agrees that location is vital to the success of the operation. He has seen some distinct exceptions to the rule, but overall location can make all the difference. "You have to make sure you have the right concept in the right place," he says. "When restaurants close it's often because they have the wrong concept for their neighborhood, for example opening a fine-dining restaurant in a working class area. It's like trying to put a square peg in a round hole. Understanding your market is important."

If you feel confident that you are opening the right concept at the right location, the next essential ingredient for success is talent. "Your talent is the brand," Ponce says. "You have to have great talent from the chef to the general manager and support staff." Ponce says that is why hiring the right people is so important.

Ponce also puts a lot of emphasis on leadership skills. "You cannot be a leader and have a narrow perspective," says Ponce. "If the business is doing poorly most leaders find it easier to deal with costs. They reduce portion sizes, get lesser-grade foods, or reduce customer service. But the real question to answer is how to get more sales." Being a leader, says Ponce, you have to be open to looking at all aspects of the business. If you have not had formal leadership training, then it is critical for you to develop leadership skills as soon as possible. Ponce recommends reading books on the subject or viewing videos by speakers like internationally known management consultant Tom Peters online. Ponce says he has learned that there are five nonnegotiable skills needed to be an effective leader: vision, passion, integrity, trust, and courage.

On the practical side of the business, experts agree that the success of a business can often boil down to how well it is capitalized. "You have to make sure there is capital available when times are tough," Ponce says. "My gut reaction is that it all boils down to who has the best capitalization with the strongest business plan," notes Cohen. "The business is thriving, but adjustments to business models are definitely occurring. Starbucks is cutting back stores. Dunkin' Donuts is increasing its product line." It is about being nimble and adjusting to customer demand and flow.

"Take a good hard look at operations," says Cohen. "You have to be savvy enough to understand where to cut back and not impact the customer's experience." Cohen uses the example of steak. Instead of using the most expensive cut, use a less expensive cut and put the extra effort into preparing it in a way that is just as flavorful as the more expensive version.

Finally, there is the matter of ethics. Grote says that after 45 years in the business his philosophy has never changed. "Do it right or not at all," he says. "Always do the right thing. You will build credibility, trust, and loyalty. Donatos was founded on a simple philosophy: to make the best pizza and to treat others the way you would like to be treated. This is goodwill and this philosophy is still the driving force behind everything we do at Donatos, both in our restaurants and in the communities we serve."

Edna Morris, CEO of Genshai Ollin, is an industry veteran of more than 30 years. Morris says community service is very important to the success of a restaurant and for an entrepreneur's own personal growth. "Get into some aspect of public service that you like," she says. "Find your niche and spend as much time there as you can." But she also says to not forget to spend time in your base business as well, learning every facet of the operation you can. "There is no substitute for spending time in your base business," she says. "Learn everything you need to know, even if you specialize in human resources or marketing. Everything you do will be more impactful because you know the business."

She also advises operators to remain a student. "Stay curious," she says. "Never think you've learned it all, and use every opportunity to network in similar and different fields."

Chapter 5

Talk Like a Pro

From culinary terms and kitchen equipment, to food safety, point of sales systems, and marketing and accounting terms, discussing the food services industry with other professionals can often end up sounding like a foreign language to those not familiar with all the terminology. Nothing is worse than being the butt of jokes or getting an assigned task wrong the first few days on-the-job because you did not want to admit you did not understand what someone was saying.

Take a few moments to read through this in-depth glossary of terms. And remember to use it as a handy reference guide in the future. You never know when a "new" term might be mentioned on the job. And experts agree, in this industry you will always be learning something new.

accreditation Certain jobs in the food services industry can require accreditation or employers will prefer to hire accredited employees for them. One example is a baker, who can become accredited through the Retailer's Bakery Association. Accreditation is often achieved through written and hands-on tests.

actual cost pricing This method for determining menu prices is most often used by caterers. It takes the total budget amount and divides it into percentages for labor, overhead, food cost, and profit. The four percentages must equal 100 percent.

add-on items Primarily used in restaurants, these are menu items that customers order in addition to their entrée such as salads, beverages, and desserts.

airline food service A subsegment of the transportation food services segment, the retail sales equivalent for airlines is defined as the value of all meals, including nonalcoholic beverages, on domestic and international flights originating in the United States. Technomic calculates the number of meals as a function of the number of revenue passenger miles flown in the United States by domestic and foreign airline carriers.

à la carte Applicable to all types of food service operations, à la carte is a menu or portion of a menu on which each item is ordered separately and has its own price.

all other retailers The "all other retailer" segment represents sales of food and nonalcoholic beverages for immediate consumption at establishments in general merchandise stores such as Sears and Kmart, in drug stores such as Walgreens, and in other retail hosts like liquor stores. Sales of food and beverages at convenience stores and supermarket in-store delis are looked at as separate categories. In addition to major national organizations, small chains and independents are also included.

allumette A kitchen term that refers to a knife cut often used for potatoes. The slices measure 1/4 inch by 1/4 inch by 2 1/2 inches.

all-you-care-to-eat A segment of the restaurant industry in which customers prepay a flat rate, and then have access to the dining area where the food is available in unlimited supply.

Alsace A region of France located on the German border that originated Franco-German cuisine adopted by the United States and other countries, such as quiche.

Apicius This is the name of the Roman citizen credited as the author of the first cookbook ever written, in the first century.

apprentice In an apprenticeship, students work full time under a master chef and go to school part time. They are paid salaries. Many programs, like the one through the American Culinary Federation (http://www.acfchefs.org) offer apprenticeships.

area treatment The design and décor of the areas of a restaurant or cafeteria where food is served.

artisan breads Artisan breads is the term used for breads that were originally created internationally by skilled bakers. They may take training and skill to successfully bake, especially on a consistent basis. In the United States artisan breads achieved amazing popularity in the 1990s, and are still very popular at bakeries and restaurants today. Many of them are now well-known breads like foccacias and baguettes.

artisan wines Similar to artisan breads, this term refers to wines that originated outside the United States, most often in European countries by specially trained or educated winemakers. These wines are usually the product of skilled winemakers.

as purchased This kitchen term refers to the weight of a food product, typically a cut of meat, before trimming or removal of unwanted parts.

assembly/serve system Used most commonly in cafeteria or non-restaurant settings, fully prepared foods are stored, assembled, and reheated.

au gratin oven Also known as a finishing oven, this piece of kitchen equipment is an oven with a hinged door attached to the top of a broiler.

back of the house This term is also written and spoken as "back-of-house," and refers primarily to all operations and employees in a restaurant or food services establishment that take place or work in the kitchen or away from the public eating area.

bain-marie A kitchen term that can refer to a hot water bath or the vessel used for the hot water bath. The hot water bath is used to keep foods hot.

baker's table This table for the kitchen is usually built with raised sides or curbing, usually four to six inches tall that reduces flour spillage during the baking process. It may also have tilt out bins for ingredient storage.

banquet cart This mobile piece of equipment is typically used for buffet-style dining. This cart may be insulated or non-insulated and typically comes equipped with shelving or racks for plates, and an electrically powered heating or refrigeration device.

bar corkboard This term refers to the under-counter workspace in bars. It is also known as a sink workboard and it contains sinks, drain boards, cocktail mix stations, ice storage chests, beverage coolers, and glass washers.

bars and taverns Considered a category of the food services industry, the United States Census Bureau defines them as "establishments known as bars, taverns, night clubs, or drinking places primarily engaged in preparing and serving alcoholic beverages for immediate consumption. These establishments may also provide limited food services." Technomic, a food services consulting and research company, says that bars and taverns represent the smallest primarily commercial segment of the industry.

batonnet A kitchen term that refers to a knife cut that measures 1/2 inch by 1/2 inch by 2 1/2—3 inches. The uniformity of slices makes a dish more attractive and assures more even cooking.

Beard, James A well known authority in food services, he is the author of many books, had his own catering business and restaurant, and was the first person in the industry to have a television show. He died in 1985. Since then the James Beard Foundation of New York awards chefs, food and beverage professionals, broadcast media, journalists, and authors working on food, and restaurant architects and designers awards that are so prestigious they have been called the Oscars for the food industry by *Time* magazine.

béchamel A cooking term that refers to a basic white sauce made of milk, butter, and flour (roux). It is the basis for many other sauces such as Mornay sauce.

beef cart A mobile cart used for keeping meat at serving temperature in the dining room while a server or other employee slices it for customer consumption.

beer system A method used in some restaurants or bars for beer dispensing. The kegs of beers are kept in a refrigerated location and a system of pressurized, insulated, and refrigerated lines transports it to dispensers at the bar.

biological hazard Not just a medical term, in the food services industry this term refers to the potential contamination of food by pathogenic microorganisms.

blanch A cooking process usually used for fruits or vegetables. The food product is immersed in boiling water for a brief period of time. Sometimes this process is followed by an immersion in ice to stop the cooking process.

blast chiller A refrigeration unit that circulates cold air. The benefit to using it is that it can reduce the temperatures of hot foods very quickly.

bolster A kitchen term that refers to a part of cooking knives. The bolster is the part of the knife that joins the blade to the handle. Its purpose is to add weight and balance, keeping the chef's hand steady.

bottle trough A bar term that refers to the trough mounted to the bar work board where frequently used bottles of alcohol and mixers are kept.

boulangerie A term that originated in France, it refers to a bakery that specializes in bread and rolls.

bouquet garni A French cooking term that refers to a bundle of herbs tied together and put into a pot to boil for stock or soups. They are then removed before the dish is served. There is no one recipe for bouquet garni, it may vary according to the dish it is seasoning. A soup garni may consist of herbs such as basil, burnet, thyme, chervil, rosemary, peppercorns, savory, and tarragon.

branded concept A term that refers to an operation's marketing campaign. This is a campaign that communicates an identifiable and consistent brand to consumers over time.

branded product costs An accounting term for franchisees, this refers to the costs of products it is necessary to buy to maintain the franchise or license agreement.

breading machine A piece of kitchen equipment that coats food items with breading mix.

brix A kitchen term that refers to the percentage of sugar in a product that contains syrup or other sugar solution.

broadline distributor A distributor that carries a complete and broad line of products to serve the food service industry including dry grocery, frozen, tabletop, equipment and supplies. Some broadliners carry perishable food items such as meat, dairy, and produce. A typical broadline distributor can carry 8,000 to 12,000 stock-keeping units. In addition to products broadliners also offer credit terms and other services that can add value to the food service operator.

broker A wholesaler who brings buyers and sellers together.

brunoise A name for a knife cut that produces small, uniform pieces, measuring 1/8 inch by 1/8 inch by 1/8 inch.

buffalo chopper A piece of kitchen equipment that is used to finely chop food items. Food can be either cooked or raw.

business and industry This is a segment of the food services industry that feeds employees in offices, factories, and plants. According to Technomic, a large extent of this service is handled by contract feeding companies such as ARAMARK, Service America, and Canteen.

bussing A word used to describe the act of clearing away used plates and silverware from a table in a restaurant dining area. Sometimes this job also entails preparing the table for the next customer.

buying groups Companies that consolidate purchases and provide support for their distributor members. Most often small, medium, and even some large broadline distributors are members of a buying group. Technomic says most buying groups carry their own members' distributor-label products.

by-the-ounce This is a strategy employed by several restaurants in different segments. Customers prepare their own salads, soups, or other foods and are charged by the ounce. Other restaurants use this strategy for steaks. The customer chooses the cut of steak and is charged by the ounce.

cafeterias/buffets According to the United States Census Bureau, this segment of the food services industry consists of food service operations that serve patrons in a continuous line. The menu consists of various foods that are prepared and ready as customers move through the cafeteria line.

caramelization Cooking term that refers to foods with high sugar content that are cooked at high temperatures, usually 300 degrees or higher, to release the sugars and brown.

casual dining restaurant The casual dining restaurant is a subsegment of the full-service segment. In full-service restaurants, patrons receive table service, versus ordering at a counter. In casual dining restaurants, establishments have

Fast Facts

Why Are So Many Culinary Terms French?

Over the years French culinary terms have become Anglicized to the point that many people do not realize they are derived from the French term, such as fillet and entrée. The reason these French cooking terms have become engrained into our language is due primarily to Frenchman Auguste Escoffier, who published what was at the time considered the most important cookbook, *The Culinary Guide*, in the early 1900s. Included in this widely read book were French cooking techniques and terms.

table service, full bar service, and focus on lunch and dinner dayparts. Check averages are between $10 and $25 per person.

chain/multiunit operators Chain or multiunit companies are those that operate more than 10 food service establishments and maintain some degree of centralized control. Chain/multiunit operators manage both commercial and noncommercial establishments.

chapati A flatbread that originated in India and which cooked on a hot griddle.

check averages Used as a measurement and defining factor most often in the food services industry, this term refers to the average dollar amount of checks at a particular restaurant.

chemical hazard Applicable to all food services operations, this term refers to the potential contamination of food by other chemicals found in an operation's facilities such as cleaners and pesticides.

colleges and universities Colleges and universities represent a market in the food services industry. Included in this group are public and private two-year and four-year colleges and junior college programs. The key food service areas are board contracts in dormitories, cafeterias, snack shops, and special function services.

combi-ovens These ovens offer a bit more versatility; they can cook foods with dry/convection heat or steam heat.

comfort foods Menu items intended to remind customers of old-fashioned, traditional, home-cooked American meals.

commercial establishments In the industry this term refers to public establishments, which could be housed in freestanding buildings or included in or part of another establishment, with the objective of preparing, serving, and selling meals and snacks for profit to the general public. This is how this part of the industry is distinguished from noncommercial establishments.

commissary system Used primarily by food service operations with multiple locations, a central production kitchen controls the cooking and food supply and delivers the food to the other locations.

contract food services Used most commonly by non-restaurant operations, this refers to companies that offer cafeteria or food services to their employees, but have contracted with outside vendors to supply the food and/or service.

convenience store (petroleum-based)   Convenience stores represent a portion of the food services industry, because they often sell and serve food and beverages. Technomic further breaks this category into petroleum based, and traditional convenience stores. The petroleum based segment consists of convenience stores that are part of gas stations.

convenience store (traditional)   Higher margin grocery stores that do not have a broad inventory or product offering and are not part of gas stations.

conventional supermarket   Supermarkets are considered part of the food services industry when they sell ready to eat foods in delis or bakeries. Technomic, a fact-based research and food services consulting firm says supermarkets offer a full line of groceries, meat, and produce and earn at least $2 million in annual sales. These stores typically carry at least 9,000 items. Most of these full-service stores also offer a service deli and bakery.

conveyor ovens   Ovens used frequently for pizzas and subs, they are set at one temperature and a conveyor belt moves the food through the oven so it is consistently baked each time.

cook/chill method   A cooking method most commonly used in institutions such as hospitals and prisons, food is prepared by conventional methods and then chilled or refrigerated until time for use.

cook/freeze   A cooking method used in institutions such as prisons or other non-restaurant food service preparations, like cook/chill or ready/prepared, food is prepared by conventional methods and then chilled or refrigerated until time for use.

cook-hold oven   An oven that cooks foods slowly. The benefit of this is that the food retains more moisture, shrinks less, and is more flavorful.

costing   An important part of budgeting, forecasting, and planning, this is the process used to determine an operation's costs and potential profits.

critical control point   Part of the HACCP food safety process, any point in a food system where loss of control could pose an unacceptable health risk.

cross-contamination   In kitchens cross-contamination can occur when bacteria in one food is transferred to others through cutting boards, knives, unclean countertops, or hands.

C-stores Another name for cash and carry convenience stories.

custom sandwich A menu item that allows customers to custom build their sandwiches from a published list of ingredients. Usually the term refers to cold sandwiches only.

cycle menu A strategy of many restaurants, usually ones in the full-service segment, in which a set of planned menus is cycled through during regular time periods such as winter, spring, and fall.

danger zone In the food services industry this term refers to the United States Food and Drug Administration's determination that foods at temperatures between 41 and 140 degrees are at higher risk for contamination. It was found that bacteria rapidly multiply in foods in this range of temperatures.

dayparts In the food services industry this term refers to the various meal times throughout the day, such as breakfast, lunch, and dinner dayparts. Not all restaurants serve customers during all of these dayparts. Dayparts are viewed as different markets for restaurants.

direct subsidy Restaurant accounting term which refers to money used to offset the difference between food service sales and expenses.

display cooking This term refers to a restaurant design, first started in California where the kitchen and food preparation is visible to the patrons; also known as open kitchen design.

drug stores Drug stores can be considered part of the food services industry when they sell food products. A drug store is defined by the United States Census Bureau as an establishment that sells prescription drugs. It may also sell a variety of additional items related to health care, beauty and skin care products, and other household items. Some of these establishments may also feature a soda fountain or lunch counter.

du jour menu Many operations offer this current day menu, giving the operation the opportunity to provide seasonal or more creative or profitable fare.

dunnage rack A platform used to store cases or bags of food in a cold storage unit or storeroom. The platform may be mobile or stationary, solid or louvered.

durable equipment Restaurant equipment that becomes a permanent part of the facilities. This term can refer to equipment used in service, preparation, or storage of food.

ECR Electronic cash registers that also maintain data of all products sold.

edible portion This is a kitchen term that refers to the weight of a menu item after it has been trimmed, prepared, and cooked.

Escoffier, Auguste The name of a French chef who lived in the late 1800s through the early 1900s who revolutionized the workings of kitchens and created many famous recipes such as Peach Melba. He also wrote the book *The Culinary Guide* in 1903.

expendable equipment This term refers to small items used in food services that are frequently lost or broken and will need to be frequently replaced. Examples of these items are plates, silverware, and kitchen utensils.

factor pricing A method for determining menu pricing. This method takes your target food-cost percentage (how much you want to make on this item, most establishments target a percentage of 10 to 20 percent), and divide it into 100. For example if you want to make a 20 percent profit, take 20 and divide it into 100. Your factor is 5.00. Then you multiply this factor by the actual food cost of an item. If the cost of a steak on your menu is $3.00, multiply it by your factor $5.00 and the menu price of that item is $15.00.

family value marketing A pricing strategy in restaurants or other food service established aimed to appeal to parents' budgets.

FF&E Abbreviation that stands for furniture, fixtures, and equipment in a food service operation.

fine-dining restaurant A subsegment of the full-service segment, these establishments emphasize dinner and check averages are typically more than $20 per person. These restaurants are also known as white tablecloth restaurants.

first-in-first-out Used by a variety of food services organizations, this is a food inventory method that is used to ensure that products are used in the order they arrive at the location.

flow of food This term applies to all food service operations, and refers to, from start to finish, how food enters a restaurant or food service operation, and the path leading to its final destination.

food cost percentage pricing A method for determining menu pricing. Of all the pricing methods, this one is the most widely used. It takes the price of an item and divides it by the target food cost percentage. For example if you have a burger on your menu that costs you $1.00 to prepare, and your target food cost percentage (how much you want to make on this item, most establishments target a percentage of 10 to 20 percent) is 25 percent, $1.00 divided by 25% = $4.00.

food merchandiser Used frequently by restaurants that sell items for customers to take home like desserts or other baked goods, or by cafeteria-style restaurant formats, this term refers to refrigerated or heated cabinets with glass doors or ends.

Foodservice Management Firms or Contract Feeders This term refers to companies that operate and manage food service facilities within and/or for other establishments (usually noncommercial establishments like prisons) for the purpose of making a profit.

forecasting The estimate of the quantity of food needed for a day or other specified time period.

front of the house This term is also written and spoken as "front-of-house," and refers primarily to all operations and employees in a restaurant or food services establishment that take place or work in the public eating area.

full-service restaurants Restaurants that offer a relatively broad menu along with table, counter, and/or booth service. Customers are waited on at their tables rather than walking to order counters. These establishments primarily offer meals for immediate consumption at their locations, but customers can also order food for take-out.

garde manger This entry-level position in the kitchen is responsible for preparing cold foods.

general merchandise stores These businesses are sometimes included in the food services category when they sell food. The United States Census Bureau defines these stores as retail stores that sell a broad variety of products across a number of categories, including dry goods, clothing, furniture, house wares, hardware, and food. Variety stores, department stores, and warehouse clubs are included in this category. According to Technomic, general merchandise stores and drug stores are often combined to form the general merchandise/drug segment.

grade In the food services industry meats, poultry, and eggs are given grades to designate their quality. The higher the quality of the product, the higher the grade will be.

gray water This is a kitchen term that refers to wash water and other water that is disposed of through sink drains.

gremolata This kitchen term refers to a condiment that is made with minced parsley, garlic, and lemon zest. It is usually paired with veal but also goes well with fish and seafood.

gross margin Accounting term that indicates the amount derived by subtracting the unit cost from the unit price, or total cost from total price.

gross-profit pricing This method of menu pricing is appropriate for established organizations with several months of history, and after an item has been on the menu prior to knowing its actual costs. This is calculated using the following information: past revenue in dollars, past gross profit in dollars, past number of customers, and the item's actual food cost. The revised menu cost is determined by dividing the gross profit by the number of customers. The result is an average gross profit per customer. Add the average gross profit per customer to the item's actual food cost and the final result is its menu price.

group purchasing organizations Organizations of the food services industry whose main function is to consolidate purchases and provide support for their food service distributor members. Most small, medium, and even some large broadline distributors are members of a group purchasing organization. Additionally, most GPOs carry their own members' distributor-label products.

hazard analysis Used in all food service operations, this is a system for food safety that details safe food handling procedures and potential hazards to food safety. It identifies potential food safety hazards so that key actions known as Critical Control Points (CCPs) can be taken to reduce or eliminate risks of hazards occurring. (*See* critical control points.)

home meal replacements Becoming a more popular strategy at many restaurants in all segments, menu offerings designed by restaurants that families can take home and eat together.

indirect subsidy An accounting term that includes all the costs of operating a facility, including rent, security, property taxes, insurance, and other overhead.

in-house management Mainly used in food service operations other than restaurants, this term primarily refers to facilities that own and operate their own food service departments. For example, a hospital or large company that provides cafeteria services to its employees.

julienne A commonly used knife cut, slices measure 1/8 inch by 1/8 inch by 2 1/2 inches.

just-in-time inventory control Used in many food services operations, this is an inventory management system that looks at suppliers' and customers' demands over time and works to reduce inventory costs.

kitchen brigade system This is a term that refers to a method of organizing kitchen staff members created by Auguste Escoffier, a French chef in the late-1800s and still used by most food services establishments today. It is an organizational chart for the kitchen, and defines jobs and a chain of command with the chef at the top of the hierarchy.

K-minus Industry term used to refer to a food service facility that does not contain a kitchen. Instead a central kitchen prepares the food and transports it to the facility.

layout Used primarily in kitchens, this refers to a plan for equipment placement in a given room.

limited service restaurant Establishments whose patrons generally order or select items and pay before eating. Food and drink may be consumed on premises, taken out, or delivered to customers' locations. Note: This segment consists of quick-service, cafeterias, and buffets.

maitre d'hotel Often shortened to maitre d', can be responsible for a wide range of duties, from seating guests, to overseeing servers, and handling customer complaints. Most often the maitre d' ensures that guests are seated as promptly and comfortably as possible and that the turnover of seating during operating hours is smooth.

manning chart A chart that graphically depicts the staffing needs of a food service operation. The chart includes job titles, functions, and time schedule.

marketing channel This term refers to the entire cycle of food delivery, from the growers of food products to the final customer ordering and receiving a menu item at the restaurant.

market segmentation Used to determine an operation's customer base, this is the process of separating customers into distinct groups based on factors such as geographic location or demographics.

matzoh A type of Jewish unleavened, baked flatbread.

meal solutions Similar to home meal replacements, a term that refers to menu items offered by restaurants that families can take home and eat together.

menu explosion Used by management or owners to determine kitchen equipment needs in new or remodeled kitchens, this is a process that calculates the amounts of food prepared for each menu item in a specific kitchen.

menu matrix A menu matrix is used to determine the amount of products sold in a restaurant, and is typically used to determine food costs.

menu pattern or meal plan This term can be used by all categories of the food services industry and refers to an outline of each menu category and the number of selections offered in each category.

mid-scale restaurant A sub-section of the full-service category, mid-scale restaurants offer table service but limited or no alcohol beverage service. Check averages are in the $6 to $10 per person range.

mirepoix A cooking term that refers to a mixture of chopped carrots, celery, and onions, which are used in many soups, stews, and sauces.

misbranded The food industry must comply with the Food and Drug Administration regulations. The FDA dictates what needs to be on the label of food products. An item is considered misbranded if the information on the label is not complete or is misleading.

modular equipment Kitchen equipment that is the same height, color, and design. Each piece can be purchased and used separately, or in various combinations.

molé A Mexican sauce concocted with many spices, vegetables, and even chocolate; it may have originated in Spain in the late 17th century, or with the Aztecs.

MTO Abbreviation for restaurants that provide menu items to their clients that are made to order.

noncommercial establishments Another term for institutional food services, this refers to all nonpublic facilities where meals and snacks are prepared and served to support the population of the facility, and not as its main source of revenue or business plan.

nonselective menu This term refers to menus that offer no choices in each category.

order wheel Metal or wood wheel with clips used by cooks and servers to track customer food orders.

organic foods The United States Food and Drug Administration defines organic produce as that which "is grown without using most conventional pesticides; fertilizers made with synthetic ingredients or sewage sludge; bioengineering; or ionizing radiation. Before a product can be labeled 'organic,' a government-approved certifier inspects the farm where the food is grown to make sure the farmer meets the U.S. Department of Agriculture's organic standards. Companies that handle or process organic food before it reaches the supermarket or restaurant must be certified too."

other noncommercial This classification of food service operations is primarily used by Technomic. It defines this category as follows: a significant number of other establishments that offer food service either for profit or in charitable establishments. This segment is composed of several small groups that usually offer some kind of food service, usually cafeteria-style. They are typically child care centers, penal institutions, or religious organizations like convents.

other retail hosts Many retail businesses sell food and beverages as a part of their business model. This segment includes miscellaneous retailers (liquor, bakeries, etc.) and does not represent a large percentage of the industry.

participation ratio This number allows operators to determine the ratio of people that are actually using the facility during any specific day part or time period. It is calculated by taking the total population in the facility's area and dividing it by the number of customers.

participation stimulators Another term for marketing or other efforts to drive more customers in the door, such as special events, sales, or offers.

pellet This term refers to a preheated metal disk that is used to maintain the temperature of an individual portion of plated hot food.

per capita spending A calculation that allows the food service operator to determine how much money each person spends at his or her operation in a given population and time period. It is calculated by taking total food sales over the specific time and dividing it by the available population.

perpetual inventory This term refers to an ongoing record of the quantities of each food product that are available in an operation's storage facilities.

personal chefs Personal chefs began making an appearance in 1991. While the term could apply to chefs that work for an individual household full time, its more recent and prevalent function is that of a chef that prepares full meals for several clients and delivers them to the homes. Personal chefs also prepare the meals in the homes of the clients.

physical inventory Food services operations often conduct a physical count of all items available in their storage facilities to make sure they match with facility records.

plate presentation A kitchen term that refers to how a dish is presented to a customer. The more well-presented an item is, the higher the customer perceives its value.

plating This is a kitchen term that refers to the process of putting a customer's food on the plate and includes adding sauces or garnish. Plating is an important part of the presentation of the meal.

poaching Kitchen term that refers to a cooking process used to prepare delicate foods like eggs or fish. The food is lightly simmered in a liquid, which can be milk, water, or broths.

point-of-sale terminals (POS) This is a combination of cash registers and computers that keeps track of items sold. Today's POS systems can provide a great deal of helpful information and safeguards.

poori A fried flatbread that originated in India.

portion-pak Small individual-size portions of condiments, such as ketchup, mustard, and mayonnaise, in disposable packaging.

potentialized food cost This calculation allows operators to determine where their food costs are exceeding their ideal costs for each item. Given an operation's menu matrix, an ideal food cost is noted for each item.

pre-portioned Food items such as meats or vegetables that are sold fully trimmed and portioned and ready to prepare.

primary market Part of the food services industry marketing channel, this is the most basic source of food supply, the growers or processors.

primary/secondary schools food service Primary/secondary schools food service encompasses all public and private primary and secondary school feeding. Total consumption is based on school purchases and government contributions, which together compose the total dollar value of food. The key components are: lunch participation, breakfast participation, milk programs, commodity contributions, and à la carte feedings.

prime cost pricing A common method for determining menu pricing, this technique takes labor costs into account. To use this method you need: total labor cost as a percentage, the labor cost for the specific menu item, actual item food cost, and target food cost as a percentage. To use this method, first add the cost of labor to prepare it to its food cost. Then determine what percentage the item's labor cost is of your total labor cost, and you have the item's labor percentage. Add this percentage to your target food cost percentage (the percent of profit you wish to make from the item). This sum is your prime food cost percentage. Divide the total item cost by the prime food cost percentage, and the result is the menu price.

prix fixe menu Menu that offers the complete meal, with everything included in one price.

production schedule This planning vehicle used by most operations is a thorough list of the menu items that will be prepared for the day, as well as a list of any advance preparation needed.

productivity rate A measurement of the productivity of a specific employee or work group. There are various ways to measure productivity, such as sales dollars achieved per labor hour or meals served per hour.

pulper A piece of kitchen equipment that grinds garbage and waste, it is usually floor-mounted.

punch list Detailed checklist of all the equipment that will go into a facility, which is then tested to ensure equipment meets specifications before the facility actually opens.

quick casual This segment of the restaurant industry is a sub-segment of the limited-service restaurant segment. Restaurants are typically attractive and comfortable, and they serve freshly prepared (or foods perceived to be freshly prepared), wholesome quality, authentic foods in a reasonably fast service format. Check averages are usually in the $6–9 per person range.

ready-prepared A cooking method most often used in institutions such as prisons, in which food is prepared by conventional methods and then chilled or refrigerated until time for consumption.

rechaud A term that refers to a small table with a small heater on it. In restaurants it is placed by customers' tables to keep hot foods hot while customers are eating other items.

recommended daily allowance (RDA) Determined by the Food and Nutrition Board of the National Academy of Sciences in Washington, D.C., this term refers to the nutrient levels

Problem Solving

Handling Customer Complaints

While most businesses depend on relationships, in the food services industry maintaining good relationships with customers is absolutely essential in order to achieve success. Here are some tips for dealing with customer complaints:

1. Listen to the customer. A server or other employee may give you his version of the story. You should keep an open mind. Do not begin thinking of solutions or responses until you fully understand the situation.

2. Once you know what happened, apologize. If it was not the fault of the restaurant, apologize anyway. Say, "I'm sorry your experience here didn't meet your expectations."

3. Sound professional. There is a fine line between a professional manner, and sounding condescending. Do not cross that line. Remain courteous even when the customer is not.

4. Lastly, it is perfectly okay to use industry-specific terms (jargon) during the conversation, if they are appropriate. If you use a term that the customer may not understand, explain it to her. But do not throw in jargon for the sake of appearances. Customers will know what you are doing, and you will be crossing that fine line again.

needed per age group and gender for a healthy, balanced diet. The RDAs determine healthy levels of vitamins and food groups.

remouillage A French cooking term that means "rewetting." Chefs use bones to make stock, and remouillage occurs when the same bones are used again to make another pot of stock.

rethermalization This cooking method refers to the process of bringing foods that have been cooked and chilled or frozen for later use back to eating temperatures.

revolving tray oven An oven that can use gas, electric, or oil heat, it contains a Ferris Wheel-like device that rotates trays of food. Trays are loaded or unloaded through one door.

roux A French cooking term that refers to the combination of fat, usually butter, and flour used to thicken sauces and soups.

running rate An accounting term for food costs, this term refers to the average, current cost of a particular item over a specific time period.

sachet A cooking term referring to a small, tied bag made out of cheesecloth and filled with herbs and spices. The sachet is dropped into pots of soups or stews for added flavor.

salad engineer A member of the wait staff who has mastered the art of carrying two fixed price self-service salads on one plate without spilling.

salamander A shelf or cabinet mounted over the back part of a range or steam table, it uses this heat to keep foods warm.

satelliting This term refers to when establishments sell or deliver food to other locations or facilities.

schedule of releases Used for staffing purposes, this schedule breaks down each day part into segments, and details the number of staff members at each segment, and when each segment is released from work.

scramble system Used primarily for cafeteria-style business models, this system separates different various points of service, such as beverage service and desserts to improve customer flow and merchandising opportunities.

secondary market This term refers to the second step in the marketing channel where food products from the primary markets are distributed to their buyers.

selective menu Most commonly used in restaurant operations, these menus offer more than one choice of food items in all of its categories.

self-operated food service An operation that is maintained and managed in-house.

semi-à la carte menus Menus that offer meals that include one or more sides, like a vegetable and salad, but other items like soups, desserts, and appetizers are sold and priced separately.

semiselective menu Used most often in restaurants, menus that offer more than one choice of food item in at least one of its categories.

servery The area in cafeteria where food is served to customers.

signature items Many restaurants or chefs build their concepts around a signature item, which is a menu item that is prepared in a way that makes it unique, and which the operation can then charge more for.

single service In food services single service refers to disposable paper products used for serving food. It includes paper plates, napkins, cups, plastic silverware, etc.

single-use menu This term refers to a menu designed for a special occasion or holiday such as Thanksgiving, most commonly occurring in restaurants, but also other segments of the industry.

small plate offerings Similar to tapas, small plate offerings are a restaurant term that refers to an alternative to ordering a full meal. Instead customers can choose a small plate of snacks that provide tastes of many menu items. The advantages are customers get to sample many menu items, and prices for the small plate offerings are typically lower than ordering a full meal.

sommelier The sommelier, or wine steward, is in charge of wines at a restaurant. The wine steward must be knowledgeable of all the many kinds of wines, vintages, and wineries and be able to discuss them with customers.

sous chef Part of the kitchen staff, the sous chef is considered second in command of the kitchen. In smaller operations, he or she may do many things. In larger establishments, he or she will direct other specialists in the kitchen.

sous vide Kitchen term referring to a production method in which food is fully cooked and then vacuum-packed.

specialty distributor In the food services industry specialty distributors distribute foods in a specific product category (e.g., meat, dairy, produce, equipment, beverages, ethnic foods, etc.) to restaurants or a specific segment (airlines, vending, etc.). Like broadline distributors they provide delivery, credit, sales representation and other value-added services. The main difference between specialty distributors and broadliners is that specialty distributors do not carry a full line of food service products. Instead they typically carry a broader and deeper line of products within their specialization categories.

spoken menu Used most often in fine-dining establishments, this is a method for communicating the menu to customers. In this method the menu is read to the customers and offers a means of servers employing suggestive selling.

spoodle This is a kitchen term that refers to a utensil used for serving food. It is a combination of a spoon and a ladle. They are often used to guarantee portion sizes.

standardized recipe As the name suggests, it is an establishment's own recipe for a particular menu item. Using standardized recipes for menu items ensures quality, consistency, cost control, makes pricing easier, helps create inventory and purchasing lists, and helps in training new employees on the item.

standards of fill The FDA's standards that detail the minimum amounts that need to be contained in each product container. These guidelines are used most often by food manufacturers and processors.

standards of identity This term refers to the FDA's guidelines for what an item needs to contain to be able to label it a certain product. For example if a product is labeled low fat, the FDA's guidelines dictate the percentage of fat it can contain to carry that label.

standards of quality The FDA's guidelines defining quality and describing the number and kinds of defects allowable in products, primarily canned fruits and vegetables.

static menu Used in many restaurants, a menu that remains the same every day.

straight line system Older, more traditional cafeteria model where customers obtain all food and beverage items in one long straight line. This is not always the most efficient system and can create long lines.

suggestive selling Used most often in full-service food services operations, suggestive selling occurs when the server in a restaurant suggests particular menu items, extras, or describes daily specials.

supermarket food service A growing number of supermarkets compete with restaurants and other segments of the food services industry by providing ready-to-eat foods, typically in deli departments. All prepared ready-to-eat or ready-to-drink products from a supermarket's deli except for bulk or unfinished items like meats, cheeses, and assembled but uncooked pizzas are considered supermarket food service. Specific deli products classified as food service include beverages, desserts, fresh salads, fried or barbecued chicken, barbecued ribs, hot prepared entrees, sandwiches, yogurt, tacos, soup, salads and other self-service bars. Additionally, restaurants, food bars, and kiosks operating within the store are classified as supermarket food service.

sweat This cooking term refers to a method in which vegetables are cooked in a small amount of oil and butter. Sweating is known to bring out the flavors of the vegetables, while sautéing seals them within.

systems distributor A food service systems distributor exclusively serves chain restaurants and other multi-tenant operators. They only carry the items used by their chain customers, typically only 500 to 1,000 stock-keeping units. Usually systems distributors do not provide sales representation for the products they carry.

table d'hôte menu This term refers to a menu that lists and prices complete meals.

tapas Although tapas have been around in Spain for many years, they are a relatively new trend in the United States. Tapas refer to an order of small bites of food that are typically served with alcoholic beverages. They can be anything from cheeses, olives, and cured meats, to tuna. They differ from appetizers in one important aspect: they are not meant to be a prelude to an entrée, but to be eaten with the drink until the person is full.

tempered Frozen foods that are thawed by placing them in the refrigerator. This can also refer to a technique of slowly adding hot liquids to cold ingredients and is done so the cold items will not curdle.

toque blanche The French term used universally for the chef's hat.

transportation food service Transportation food service is a segment of the food services industry that primarily refers to airlines and other transportation companies that serve food as part of their services.

upscaled menus Usually used in fine-dining restaurants, menu items are designed to appeal to gourmets, usually with more expensive ingredients.

vended food service A food service facility where all food is dispensed through automatic merchandising equipment.

vending The vending market is defined as all food and beverage products sold through automatic vending machines, regardless of their location. Not included are other vended products such as cigarettes, cigars, bulk vending, and other nonfood items.

verbal menus Another term for spoken menus, used by some fine-dining establishments. Verbal menus are where servers verbally present the day's options to guests. This gives the servers opportunities for suggestive selling.

whole foods Often confused with organic foods, whole foods are not necessarily organic, and vice versa. The term refers to foods that are unprocessed and unrefined, or minimally processed or refined.

yield test Yield tests are most often conducted by restaurants and food processors, and determine how much of a food product is edible after it is prepared and how much is discarded.

Chapter 6

Resources

Thanks to the World Wide Web, there has been a veritable explosion of resources available to newbies of any field, including food services. From trade associations, Web sites, and publications, to schools and universities, there is a wealth of resources today that can keep you competitive and help you succeed in this exciting, extremely fast-paced industry. These sources provide information such as job postings, human resources forms, laws and regulations of the industry, and food safety issues. The difficulty lies in choosing the right sources for you. Once you have determined a career path and area of specialization, resources supporting this choice are plentiful. Here are the most well-known resources available to those in the food services industry today.

Associations and Organizations

While association fees can be expensive, the benefits of joining at least one can far exceed the costs involved. The size of the organization's membership often determines the extent and quality of its benefits, but most associations offer continuing education, seminars, networking, and an annual conference. They also usually keep up with the latest news and trends and seek to keep their members informed as well.

There are trade associations for every facet of the food services industry. Here are the most prominent associations for each industry segment.

Food Service Providers

Commercial Food Equipment Service Association Members of this association are food equipment parts, suppliers, and service technicians. An online inventory system, certification of skills, training classes, and conferences are also part of membership benefits. Certified members are more likely to get jobs or customers. 2216 West Meadowview Road, Suite 100, Greensboro, North Carolina, 27407, (336) 346-4700 (http://www.cfesa.com)

Food Marketing Institute Food retailers and wholesalers can join this association that develops and promotes policies and programs for its members. Food service operators will find exclusive food safety research and information, a 24/7 Crisis Hotline, and access to the industry's most comprehensive consumer and operations research services, the world's largest collection of industry resources, and a variety of print and electronic resources, good reasons to join this association. The organization also conducts and publishes research and information for the public. 2345 Crystal Drive, Suite 800, Arlington, Virginia, 22202, (202) 452-8444, (http://www.fmi.org)

Food Processing Suppliers Association This global association serves suppliers to the food, beverage, and pharmaceutical industries through market research, education, events, and industry advocates and councils. Members gain access to the largest face-to-face marketing event in the food, beverage and pharmaceutical industry in the United States, the latest market intelligence to help them more effectively make decisions for their business, and leverages the purchasing power of more than 500 member companies to obtain the best rates possible for goods and services. 1451 Dolley Madison Boulevard, Suite 101, McLean, Virginia, 22101-3850, (703) 761-2600, (http://www.iafis.org)

International Foodservice Distributors Association This association represents food service distributors throughout the United States, Canada, and internationally and has more than 170 members that provide food, equipment, and other products to restaurants and other food service providers. 1410 Spring Hill Road, Suite #210, McLean, Virginia, 22102, (703) 532-9400, (http://www.ifdaonline.org)

North American Association of Food Equipment Manufacturers More than 625 food equipment manufacturers hold membership in this association. It provides these members opportunities to showcase their latest innovations, as well as certifications, publications, and educational seminars. It also provides members the research, educational opportunities, and business forums they need to make them more competitive. 161 North Clark Street, Suite 2020, Chicago, Illinois, 60601, (312) 821-0201, (http://www.nafem.org).

Hospitality and Restaurants

American Beverage Institute ABI represents restaurants that serve adult alcoholic beverages. ABI sponsors research and educational materials involving alcohol and its effects on consumers. It also seeks to provide information on responsible adult beverage consumption to the public and policymakers. 1090 Vermont Avenue NW, Suite 800, Washington, D.C., 20005, (202) 463-7110, (http://www.bacdebate.com)

American Hotel & Lodging Association Educational resources, networking among 11,000 industry executives, and exclusive bottom line savings are some of the benefits reported by this trade association. Members also receive national advocacy on Capitol Hill, public relations and image management. The organization also offers educational materials and research. 1201 New York Avenue NW, #600, Washington, D.C., 20005-3931, (202) 289-3100, (http://www.ahla.com)

American Institute of Baking Several segments of the food processing, distribution, food services, and retail industries are served internationally by this association, through education, research, food safety education, and audit services. 1213 Bakers Way, PO Box 3999, Manhattan, Kansas, 66505-3999, (785) 537-4750, (http://www.aibonline.org)

American Institute of Wine & Food This association promotes the enjoyment of food and wine by bringing together professionals in the culinary industry with non-professionals. The primary benefit of joining is networking opportunities both locally and nationally, with well-known chefs, authors, restaurateurs, wine and food producers and purveyors, as well as other professionals and enthusiasts. Founding members include Julia Child and Robert Mondavi. AIWF also provides scholarships and educational programs. 26364 Carmel Rancho Lane, Suite 201, Carmel, California, 93923, (800) 274-2493, (http://www.aiwf.org)

Foodservice Consultants Society International, the Americas Consultants in the food service industry can become certified, take continuing education courses, keep up to date on the latest industry trends, and network with other professionals. Other members can advance their careers through professional recognition and numerous networking opportunities with colleagues. 15000 Commerce Parkway, Suite C, Mt. Laurel, New Jersey, 08054, (503) 223-9504, (http://www.fcsi.org)

Foodservice Educators Network International Culinary teachers get the opportunity to network, share ideas, and better prepare for their students through this organization. The FENI provides a forum for educators to present papers and discuss the latest concepts. 20 W Kinzie Street, Suite 1200, Chicago, Illinois, 60654, (312) 849-2220, (http://fenisummit.com)

Green Restaurant Association Teaching and encouraging restaurants to be environmentally sustainable is what this association is all about. Restaurants can earn certifications and find green suppliers and products. 89 South Street, Suite 401, Boston, Massachusetts 02111, (617) 737-3344, (http://www.dinegreen.com)

International Association of Culinary Professionals Devoted to providing continuing education and development for its more than 3,000 members worldwide, IACP scrves as a resource and support systcm for professionals in the food and beverage industry. Joining this association gives members a listing on its directory, the opportunity to purchase its mailing list, and member-to-member discounts. 1100 Johnson Ferry Road, Suite 300, Atlanta, Georgia, 30342, (404) 252-3663, (http://www.iacp.com)

International Food Service Executives Association Networking, mentoring, and community service are the primary focal points of this organization for food service industry leaders. Education, development, and certifications are also offered to members worldwide. 500 Ryland Street, Suite 200, Reno, Nevada, 89502, (775) 825-2665, (http://www.ifsea.com)

International Franchise Association The IFA protects, enhances, and promotes franchises of every business category internationally. Members include hardware stores, appliance repair, and home décor businesses as well as restaurants. 1501 K Street NW, Suite 350, Washington, D.C., 20005, (202) 628-8000, (http://franchise.org)

International Hotel & Restaurant Association This association promotes and protects the interests of hotels and restaurants worldwide through events and news reports. Members receive benefits that include access to industry best practices, networking with other

Keeping
in Touch

Networking

There are many benefits derived from networking. Let's face it though, not everyone is into doing the networking thing. Practicing and delivering a canned introduction, working the crowd, etc., can feel forced, phony, and like a lot of work. That is why experts today say lose the old mind-set of looking for people who can help your business, and instead identify people you feel you can really connect with on a personal level. Also remember to give as much as you receive. When you genuinely want to help others, they are more likely to return the favor. When you relax and enjoy the experience instead of forcing it, here's what you can gain:

- At the least new friendships with those you may not have met elsewhere
- Relationships with others interested in your industry that can give you a new perspective
- Connections with other companies in your industry
- First knowledge of jobs and promotions at other companies
- Pass-it-forward opportunities—if they cannot help you, they may know someone who can

executives, and other benefits. 87, rue Montbrillant, 1202 Geneva, Switzerland, +41 22 734 80 41, (http://www.ih-ra.com)

National Ice Cream Retailers Association Ice cream and frozen dessert retailers can network at the association's annual conference, share promotional and marketing ideas, take part in continuing education, and receive the latest news and other benefits of this organization. 1028 West Devon Avenue, Elk Grove Village, Illinois, 60007, (847) 301-7500, (http://www.nicra.org)

National Restaurant Association This association is the nation's largest for the restaurant industry, and has more than 380,000 member restaurants. Legislative representation, access to important research that impacts your operations and bottom line, top rated professional training and education, and tools and resources are included in member benefits. 1200 17th Street NW, Washington, D.C., 20036, (202) 331-5900, (http://www.restaurant.org)

U.S. Personal Chef Association This relatively new segment in the food services industry (it started in 1989) is supported by this association offering training, certification, insurance, menu planning software, and equipment. 610 Quantum, Rio Rancho, New Mexico, 87124, (800) 995-2138, (http://www.uspca.com)

Women Chefs & Restaurateurs Started by some of the top women chefs in the industry, this association seeks to promote and enhance the role of women in the restaurant industry. Members gain access to job banks, research, discounts, and more. P.O. Box 1875, Madison, Alabama, 35758, (877) 927-7787, (http://www.womenchefs.org)

Institutional or Noncommercial Food Service

The National Association of College & University Food Services The NACUFS provides its more than 600 members educational opportunities, technical assistance, scholarships, industry information, a jobs bank, and research. 525 Jolly Road, Suite 280, Okemos, Michigan, 48864-3680, (517) 332-2494, (http://www.nacufs.org)

The School Nutrition Association Formerly the American School Food Service Association, the SNA's more than 55,000 members receive benefits that include education and training, certification, and legislative representation. The association represents the nutritional needs of all children. Members can enhance and further their careers through SNA Certification and Credentialing, and increase their wealth of knowledge with professional development materials and up-to-date industry news. 700 South Washington Street, Suite 300, Alexandria, Virginia, 22314, (703) 739-3900, (http://schoolnutrition.org)

The Society for Foodservice Management The goal of this association for on-site cafeterias in corporations, hospitals, and other locations is to enable its members to achieve their career and business objectives through networking, research, publications, and other member benefits. A membership directory, regional events, and advertising and sponsorship opportunities are also available. 15000 Commerce Parkway, Suite C, Mount Laurel, New Jersey, 08054, (856) 380-6829, (http://www.sfm-online.org)

Books and Periodicals

Books

Bond's Top 50 Food-Service Franchises. By Robert E. Bond (Source Book Publications 2009). Primarily targeted at investors, this book offers an in-depth analysis of 50 top restaurant franchises, ranked according to financial growth and stability, historical performance, and owner and customer satisfaction.

Careers in the Food Services Industry (Success Without College). By Robert K. Otterbourg (Barron's Educational Series, Inc., 1999). Featuring more than 25 profiles of people who have successfully entered the food service industry, this practical guide outlines the most efficient pathways to culinary careers. It contains a wealth of information on topics such as pay scales, the processes of job recruitment, and how to complete a successful apprenticeship.

Food Jobs: 150 Great Jobs for Culinary Students, Career Changers and Food Lovers. By Irena Chalmers (Beaufort Books, 2008). Covering everything from the obvious (chef) to the more obscure (wild game hunter), this book provides a thorough introduction to a wide variety of culinary careers. Those who may feel a calling to the field, but are unsure of where to begin or how to channel their energies, are advised to seek out this book. It also features detailed interviews with experienced professionals, such as food historian Betty Fussell and Stonewall Kitchens founder Jonathan King.

Opportunities in Culinary Careers. By Mary Donovan (McGraw-Hill, 2008). Another fine introduction to the opportunities of the culinary world, this volume covers a range of careers, with a specific focus on self-employment in jobs such as private caterer or lunch stand owner. Potential work settings are described in detail, such as restaurants, food testing labs, and nursing homes. The volume also includes a thorough resource section for information on professional apprenticeships and educational programs.

Opportunities in Food Service Careers. By Caprione Chmelynski (VGM Career Horizons, 1999). This introduction to the various jobs in the food service industry serves as an excellent primer for those just beginning to investigate the field. The author discusses each career in detail, from educational requirements to salary information to descriptions of the day-to-day tasks involved in the job.

Periodicals

Busy professionals in this fast-paced industry may have difficulty finding time to read, but if you want to maintain a competitive edge, you will have to do so. Innovations in menus and menu items, service, equipment, technology, and business practices occur almost daily. Taking advantage of these innovations can make one operator or manager more successful than others in the same market. In addition to the latest changes, these publications also offer news, job

Problem
Solving
Keeping Up with Industry News and Trends

A career in the food services industry often means working long hours with little sleep or time for reading. But staying informed of the latest trends and news is critical for building success. Here are some time-saving ways to stay on top of the informational curve.

- E-newsletters: E-newsletters like the National Restaurant Association's Smart Brief are free and open to anyone—you do not have to be a member. Other food services Web sites like Foodservice-central.com also offer free e-newsletters with a free membership. Each day as you check your e-mail you can also take a few minutes to scan the latest news.

- Podcasts: The Podcast Grill interviews executives and movers and shakers in the restaurant industry. You can also download the podcasts at iTunes and PodcastAlley.com. Once you download them, listen to them on the train, bus, as you walk to work, or during a break. *Nation's Restaurant News* and *Restaurants and Institutions* are among other publications and Web sites that also offer podcasts. (http://podcastgrill.wordpress.com)

- RSS feeds: Restaurant News Resource offers the latest industry news, trends, and job openings in a variety of formats. You can subscribe to its RSS feed using Live Bookmarks, download to your PDA, or request the news in a daily e-mail. Read at your convenience. (http://www.restaurantnewsresource.com)

listings, articles on food safety and government policy issues, and other useful information.

Most publications offered by trade associations are part of the member benefit package. Other industry magazines offer free subscriptions to those who qualify. As long as you are a member of the publication's target market, you should get your subscription at no charge. Here are the leading publications in each industry segment.

Food Service Providers

Foodservice Equipment & Supplies. Distributed monthly for dealers and distributors of food service equipment and supplies and for those who design food service facilities, this magazine reports on industry trends, forecasts, and people and events. (http://www.fesmag.com)

Foodservice Equipment Reports. Supplies objective reviews and evaluations of equipment and supplies. It also publishes in-depth coverage of distribution and specification channels and a yearly buyer's guide. It is published monthly. (http://www.fermag.com)

Hospitality Design. This magazine publishes ten times a year and includes information about renovation, design, and construction of restaurants, hotels, resorts, cruise ships, and other hospitality-oriented locations. (http://www.hdmag.com)

Hospitality Technology. This magazine can provide reviews, reports, and information on the latest technology in the field and what it can do for restaurants' bottom line. It prints 10 issues a year. (http://www.htmagazine.com)

NAFEM in Print. This is a quarterly publication of the North American Association of Food Equipment Manufacturers. Its goal is to provide comprehensive coverage of the industry. Its sister publication, *NAFEM for Operators,* publishes articles on the latest equipment trends and news for operators in the food services industry.

Hospitality and Restaurants

Chain Leader. Turn here for information about managing restaurant chains at the corporate headquarters level. The monthly magazine discusses topics like finances, human resources, leadership, and brand management. (http://www.chainleader.com)

Chef. This magazine is written for culinary professionals, with ideas for new menu items, keeping kitchen costs down, and using seasonal ingredients. *Chef* publishes eleven issues per year. Its sister publication, *Chef Educator Today,* serves the teaching culinary professional and is the official publication of the Foodservice Educators Network International. (http://www.chefmagazine .com); (http://www.chefedtoday.com)

The Consultant. This is published by the Foodservice Consultants Society International for its members. Articles are written by members and key industry professionals. The Society also publishes presentations and conference material in this quarterly magazine. (http://www.fcsi.org/the_consultant.htm)

Cornell Hospitality Quarterly. This is an academic journal of Cornell University publishing research in the field of hospitality management. It also publishes case studies and industry perspectives. (http:// www.hotelschool.cornell.edu/research/chr/pubs/quarterly/)

Fast Casual. This magazine serves the fast casual restaurant segment by reporting on specific departments each issue. These departments include new concepts, fastest brands, menu concepts, restaurant design, metrics, statistics, and marketing ideas. (http:// www.fastcasual.com)

Food and Drink. This magazine's readers are CEOs, executives, and leaders of restaurant, food processing, manufacturing, service, and distribution companies. Articles present ideas of best practices in many facets of operations, including supply chain management, productivity, and food safety. (http://www.fooddrink-magazine .com)

Hotel F&B. Targets hotel, resort, and casino food services operators, one of the largest sectors of the industry. This bimonthly publication "covers profitable and effective strategies in the development, operation, and marketing of hotel food service," according to the publication's Web site. (http://www.hotelfandb.com)

My Foodservice News. This is a bimonthly national publication for independent restaurateurs and chefs. The goal of the publication is to serve as its subscribers' primary source for news and information about the food services industry. Subscribers can also receive an electronic version of the publication and a weekly e-newsletter. (http://www.mymfn.com)

Nation's Restaurant News. This is a weekly publication that brings in-depth coverage of all aspects of the industry to its readers. It looks at independent restaurants, chains, suppliers, operations, employment, and research. Subscribers can also sign up to receive e-newsletters and daily news faxes. (http://www.nrn.com)

Pizza Magazine. This is published by Pizza Marketing Quarterly. The goal of both media is to provide marketing and promotion tips for this large sector of the industry, with more than 75,000 restaurants in the United States in 2008. *Pizza Magazine* is published monthly. (http://www.pmq.com)

Pizza Today. Presents money-making tips, ideas, marketing, restaurant management, a vendor directory, and more. This is a monthly publication of the National Association of Pizzeria Operators. (http://www.pizzatoday.com).

QSR Magazine. Serves up the news for the quick service restaurant segment. Departments include menu, operations, technology, and equipment. The magazine prints thirteen issues per year. (http://www.qsrmagazine.com)

Restaurant Business. Strives to meet the business needs of restaurant owners, whether they are independents or franchisees. The monthly magazine focuses on information that improves the bottom line from growth strategies to innovations. (http://www.restaurantbiz.com)

Restaurant Hospitality. Targets full-service restaurant operators and employees (versus fast-food chains and restaurants) as its readers. Professionals at hotels, motels, fast casual restaurants, and clubs will find information on all aspects of operating a successful business, including labor issues, menu innovations, new technologies, and emerging new concepts. (http://www.restauranthospitality.com).

Restaurants & Institutions. Readers find business-critical information in this publication. This monthly magazine provides information on the broadest range of food services segments: noncommercial organizations, hospitals, convenience stores, supermarkets, and hotels, as well as independent restaurants and chains. (http://www.rimag.com)

Restaurant Startup & Growth. Readers are entrepreneurs in the industry. This monthly publication features start-up profiles, case studies, start-up resources, menu ideas, chef training, and more. (http://www.rsgmag.com)

Slammed. Shares in-depth restaurant industry expertise through expert-led roundtables, guest columnists, and business profiles. It offers more than a discussion of problems—it proposes solutions for front-of-house as well as back-of-house issues. It also features content for suppliers. (http://www.slammedmagazine.com)

Institutional or Noncommercial Food Services

Campus Dining Today. Published by the National Association of College & University Food Services this news magazine for those in college and university food services is published twice a year and serves the association's members. (http://www.nacufs.org/i4a/pages/index.cfm?pageid=3412)

Food Management. Offers operators or employees of noncommercial food services organizations helpful information. Each monthly issue contains ideas and how-to information about food and management. (http://food-management.com)

Foodservice Director. This monthly publication serves the noncommercial food service sector by reporting the latest industry news and business resources and information. (http://www.fsdmag.com)

Journal of Child Nutrition & Management. This is published by the School Nutrition Association and provides its members with the latest research and discussions on child nutrition. It is published bi-yearly. (http://docs.schoolnutrition.org/newsroom/jcnm)

School Nutrition Magazine. This is published monthly by the School Nutrition Association for its members. Professionals in school food services programs can turn to this magazine for discussions of many aspects of efficiently running their operations. (http://schoolnutrition.org/newsroom/jcnm)

Web Sites

The number one advantage to Web site viewing over accessing other forms of resources is interactivity. You are not going to get a big response from the magazine you are holding when you ask it a question. However, most of the Web sites below provide discussion forums, bulletin boards, and other means of getting almost immediate answers to your questions. Memberships to most of the sites are free and you will gain several additional benefits from joining. All of these Web sites give you access to up-to-date industry news as well as valuable tools and other information. Here are some of the leading food services industry Web sites.

DineGreen.com. As the official Web site of the Green Restaurant Association, DineGreen.com examines the most prevalent environmental problems restaurants encounter, and proposes solutions. (http://www.dinegreen.com)

Foodservice.com. This is among the original online communities for the food services industry. Daily features include job postings, a virtual food show, daily industry news and editorials, culinary schools and discussion forums. (http://www.foodservice.com)

Foodservice Central. Look here for food service community industry news, opportunities to buy and sell products online, a job marketplace, event equipment rentals, and market research. Membership includes a free e-newsletter. (http://www.foodservicecentral.com)

MonkeyDish.com. This site is owned and produced by the same company as Restaurant Business magazine. It is a customizable site loaded with useful information and tools, such as human resources forms, downloadable worksheets, templates, and video tutorials. The site also reports on the latest menu trends and posts hundreds of recipes. (http://www.monkeydish.com)

Ontherail.com. Started by a former chef and a former waiter, Ontherail.com features active news groups, bulletin boards, press information, job postings, Web site posting and free e-mail services are all part of this industry Web site. (http://www.ontherail.com)

Profitablehospitality.com. Discover free downloads of reports and articles for money-saving and profit-generating ideas for those in the hospitality business. A Members Only area provides more in-depth information. Membership rates include an up front payment plus monthly fee. (http://profitablehospitality.com)

Restaurant Doctor. From industry consultant Bill Marvin, this site offers free information, a library of resources, and schedule of industry events and programs. (http://www.restaurantdoctor.com)

RestaurantOwner.com. This is an online community of thousands of independent restaurant owners. The site contains how-to articles, training manuals, forms, business form templates, and other tools designed to aid the budding restaurateur. (http://www.restaurantowner.com)

RestaurantMarketingGroup.org. This Web site posts restaurant marketing ideas and solutions. It provides tools and support services, and membership to the organization is free. Once a member the site e-mails you marketing tips and advice. (http://www.restaurantmarketinggroup.org)

Restaurant News Resource. Find news releases, articles, interviews, stock quotes, appointments, and the latest trends related to the restaurant and hospitality industry on this site. (http://www.restaurantnewsresource.com)

RestaurantReport.com. knows that every restaurant's goal is to provide a quality dining experience. So the site posts information to aid restaurant owners, operators, managers, and staff members to do that. The site's information covers marketing, management, accounting, service, operations, public relations, and design.

Its sister site is Runningrestaurants.com, and it offers exclusive information, forms, and audio files to its members. (http://www .restaurantreport.com)

Training and Educational Resources

Getting ahead is about more than just who you know. It is also about keeping up with the latest knowledge, skills, and certifications in the industry. Continuing education is important in every field, but especially so in the ever-changing food services industry. Below is a list with descriptions of some of the top programs in the country for keeping you on the cutting edge. All information has been taken from the school, college, or university Web sites unless otherwise noted. Le Cordon Bleu Cooking schools are mentioned throughout this chapter. They are Parisian-style cooking schools that provide varying degree programs. They now offer international-based cooking techniques rather than just French techniques. Le Cordon Bleu is widely accepted in the nation and overseas as a leading culinary arts school.

Also keep in mind that the trade associations mentioned in this chapter also offer continuing education courses, seminars, and certification training. You will find that information in our listing of industry trade associations. Another source of educational information is The International Council on Hotel, Restaurant and Institutional Education, which publishes its *Guide to College Programs in Hospitality, Tourism and Culinary Arts*. The guide profiles hundreds of college programs across the country.

Here is a listing of some of the leading culinary and hospitality management programs in the nation.

Ashworth College Ashworth's online education plan offers a program in hospitality management through its school of business. The program includes lessons in all aspects of efficiently running a hotel or restaurant, including time management. It primarily focuses on day-to-day, practical job skills including managing the front and back office, coordinating guest and banquet services, banquet reservations and seating, housekeeping, marketing work flow, staffing, tourist services, scheduling, customer service and more. 430 Technology Parkway, Norcross, Georgia, 30092, (800) 957-5412, (http://www.ashworthcollege.edu).

California Culinary Academy If you are located in San Francisco and are interested in learning culinary arts, the academy teaches students the Le Cordon Bleu program. Students earn associate's degrees in the culinary arts and baking, and certificates in the culinary arts. 350 Rhode Island Street, San Francisco, California, 94103, (888) 897-3222, (http://www.baychef.com)

Cooking and Hospitality Institute of Chicago A Le Cordon Bleu school, the institute offers associate's degrees in the culinary arts and baking, and certificates in the culinary arts. It was founded in 1983 and invited to be a Cordon Bleu school in 2000. The CHIC offers quality culinary, pastry arts, and hospitality, and general education curriculums of higher education for its students. 361 West Chestnut Chicago, Illinois, 60610, (888) 295-7222, (http://www.chic.edu)

Cornell University Known worldwide as one of the best schools for hospitality management, Cornell's School of Hotel Administration offers degree programs at nearly every possible level, including doctoral degrees. Cornell also conducts industry research through its Center for Hospitality Research. 537 Statler Hall,

Fast Facts

Why should you join a trade association? Here's a list of the top reasons why joining one is a great career move:

- Networking: Meet people who can help you move up or connect you with jobs and other resources you need.

- Information: Most associations publish newsletters, journals, or magazines with the latest industry news, trends, and technologies. Many also offer seminars and conferences led by key leaders in the field.

- Advocacy: There is strength in numbers. Large associations often employ top lobbyists who advocate for new laws or revising existing laws for the betterment of the industry.

- Jobs: Several associations offer job boards, postings, or other employment services.

Ithaca, New York, 14853-6902, (607) 255-9780, (http://www
.hotelschool.cornell.edu/research/chr)

The Culinary Institute of America Hyde Park, New York, is the
main location of the CIA, where students can earn bachelor's
and associate's degrees in culinary arts. Graduates can pursue
careers as chefs, restaurant owners, managers, food writers, or
in culinary research and development. There are also branches
in California and Texas. The school offers a comprehensive program that includes an externship and 1,300 hours of hands on
training. 1946 Campus Drive, Hyde Park, New York, 12538-1499,
(845) 452-9430, (http://www.ciachef.edu)

DeVry University Students who are interested in managing hotels
or restaurants, rather than in culinary degrees, can obtain a bachelor of science degree with a concentration in hospitality management at one of DeVry's ninety locations, or take courses online.
DeVry focuses on making education easy for working adults. One
Tower Lane, Oakbrook Terrace, Illinois, 60181, (866) 338-7934,
(http://www.devry.edu)

Florida State University FSU's Dedman School of Hospitality has
been around for more than sixty years, providing the hospitality
industry with educated leaders. Students focus on one of the following programs: lodging management, conventions and events
management, food and beverage management, and club management. Its state-of-the-art facility provides hospitality students
with teaching kitchens, a satellite technology center, a publication
resource center, and a placement center. The building also contains an affiliated 35,000 square-foot, professionally managed city
club that provides hospitality students with real-world food and
beverage experience. UCB 4100, Florida State University, Talla-
hassee, Florida, 32306, (850) 644-4787, (http://cob.fsu.edu/dsh)

The Institute of Culinary Education This New York City-based
school has six-to eleven-month career training programs in culinary arts, pastry and baking arts, and culinary management. For
several years the school has been a finalist or award winner of
the International Association of Culinary Professionals' Awards
of Excellence for Culinary Schools. 50 W. 23rd Street, New York,
New York, 10010, (888) 354-2433, (http://www.iceculinary.com)

The International Culinary Center Students in New York City
can learn culinary arts or restaurant management skills in as
little as nine months (non-degree programs) at the French Culinary Institute or the Italian Culinary Academy. The school's

in-house restaurant offers students real-world kitchen and restaurant experience. 462 Broadway, New York, New York, (888)
324-2433, (http://www.internationalculinarycenter.com)
The International Culinary School at The Art Institutes The
Art Institute offers 40 locations nationwide. Degree and non-
degree programs in culinary arts, baking and pastry, hospitality
management, and food and beverage management are available.
Those looking to specialize in baking and pastry can receive an
associate's degree or certificate. Students are introduced to a variety of international recipes and culinary techniques. Culinary
learning takes place outside of the classroom through real-world
internships, student-run restaurants, enlightening guest lectures,
and opportunities to study abroad. (888) 624-0300, (http://www
.artinstitutes.edu)
Johnson and Wales University Johnson and Wales University's
two food service industry-related colleges, its Culinary Arts College and Hospitality College, work together to offer students
certificate programs and undergraduate and graduate degrees.
Whether you want to sharpen your culinary, business, marketing, or management skills, Johnson and Wales has developed
course work and programs to meet the myriad needs of a very
diverse industry. Johnson and Wales offers a unique approach
to education in this field, combining hands-on culinary training with a foundation in the liberal arts, business classes, social
responsibility and relevant work experience. This pioneering
model of education prepares students for success in today's global
economy. 8 Abbott Park Place, Providence, Rhode Island, 02903,
(800) 342-5592, (http://www.jwu.edu)
Kendall College Certificates, associate's, and bachelor's degrees in
baking and pastry arts, culinary arts, culinary management, hospitality management, hotel management, professional catering,
professional cookery, and restaurant management are offered at
this Chicago-based college. Its low student to teacher ratio and
hands-on learning experiences provide students with a balance
of practical skills and theoretical knowledge needed to excel. 900
North Branch Street, Chicago, Illinois, 60642, (888) 90.KEND-
ALL, (http://www.kendall.edu)
The Kitchen Academy There are two Kitchen Academy Locations.
Culinary students in Seattle or Sacramento will receive a fresh
approach to professional cooking. Designed by chefs, this new
culinary arts school curriculum offers an immersive concept in

culinary training delivering hands-on cooking experience. It is geared to help prepare students for a real-world culinary career. Students earn a professional culinary arts diploma. (888) 807-7222, (http://www.kitchenacademy.com)

Le Cordon Bleu Internationally known and recognized for its culinary arts programs, the school offers 14 locations around the country. It also offers programs in baking and hospitality and restaurant management. (http://culinary-school.org)

New England Culinary Institute With campuses in Montpelier and Essex Junction, Vermont, the institute offers undergraduate degrees in culinary arts and hospitality and restaurant management, as well as associate's and certificate programs. Eighty-four faculty members teach students in thirteen production kitchens. The program offers students intense personal attention from world class chef instructors and other industry professionals. The school's restaurants are the classrooms and students are expected to perform under real life working conditions from the very first day of class. 56 College Street, Montpelier, Vermont, 05602, (877) 223-NECI, (http://www.neci.edu)

Penn Foster Career School Penn Foster Career School is designed for adults who want the ability to earn a degree at their own pace and convenience. Course work is shipped to students' homes, and completed independently. Students can earn an associate's degree in hospitality management through the school and also take advantage of its career services program. 925 Oak Street, Scranton, Pennsylvania, 18515, (800) 275-4410, (http://www.pennfoster.edu)

Scottsdale Culinary Institute In Scottsdale, Arizona, Scottsdale Culinary Institute offers Le Cordon Bleu programs in culinary arts, hospitality and restaurant management, baking, and culinary management. Students receive diversified culinary training. 8100 East Camelback Road, Suite 1001, Scottsdale, Arizona, 85251, (847) 585-2731, (http://www.chefs.edu/scottsdale)

Stratford University Stratford offers a broad course offering for industry professionals. Earn a bachelor's degree in hospitality management, or associate's degrees in culinary arts, baking and pastry arts, and hotel and restaurant management at this university in Falls Church, Virginia. The school also offers a professional diploma in advanced culinary arts. 7777 Leesburg Pike, Falls Church, Virginia, 22043, (800) 444-0804, (http://www.stratford.edu)

Sullivan University With four campuses in Kentucky, Sullivan offers day, evening, weekend, and online courses for students to earn a degree. Degree programs offered at Sullivan include a bachelor of science degree in hospitality management and an associate's of science degree in hotel and restaurant management. Sullivan's advantages are small class sizes and career-focused class work. 3101 Bardstown Road, Louisville, Kentucky, 40205, (800) 844-1354, (http://www.sullivan.edu)

Texas Culinary Academy The Texas Culinary Academy offers its students Le Cordon Bleu certificates and associate's degree programs in culinary arts and baking. The school is located in Austin, Texas, and offers a unique combination of classical French cooking techniques with innovative American technology at current industry standards. 11400 Burnet Road, Suite 2100, Austin, Texas, 78758, (http://www.tca.edu)

Index